# What Others Are Saying

"Andrew and Mark have written a comprehensive, no-BS guide to dropshipping, and the candid approach it takes makes it essential reading for anyone considering this type of retail."

—**Chandra Clark**, Founder & President, Scribendi

"If you are considering getting into the dropshipping business, this is a must read. It's clear, easy to understand and unbiased. Exactly what you need to avoid all the scams out there. Highly recommended."

—**David Levin**, Author of *Don't Just Talk, Be Heard.*

"Holy jeez—I wish these guys had written this 7 years ago. I was experimenting with a dropshipping business and finding even basic info was incredibly difficult. What information I could find was either expensive or highly conflicting. As a result, I made just about every mistake in the book. Since then, I have delved deeply into worldwide logistics with another business venture and can say that the advice in this book is spot on."

—**Chris Plough**, Executive Director, MavenWire

"Dropshipping can be a very profitable addition to someone's business; however, the whole process can seem quite daunting at first. This guide is the best step-by-step instruction manual I have ever seen. Breaking it down into easy to understand components, showing you the perfect path to adding dropshipping into your business model."

—**Sharí Alexander**, Communication Specialist

"If you are thinking about starting an online business, you need this book; it's the most comprehensive guide to dropshipping I have seen. It's written by two people who have created very successful dropshipping companies, so you are learning from the masters. Their level of detail and simple step by step approach makes the complex process of dropshipping incredibly simple."

—**Jacqueline Biggs**, Author of *Marketing to Win.*

"This is by far the best book on dropshipping available. You will learn everything you need to know about finding a product, setting up an online store and growing your business."

—**Sean Work,** Director of Marketing, KISSmetrics.

"These guys distill everything you need to know about dropshipping in this comprehensive book. It's a must read if you want practical advice and a clear blueprint to help you grow your business."

—**Valerie Khoo,** National Director, Australian Writers' Centre

"This book is a must read for anyone who wants to launch an ecommerce business and get products into the hands of customers without having to invest thousands of dollars in upfront inventory. Written using real-world examples and language that's easy to understand, this entertaining and informative book includes all of the tools you'll need to successfully launch and grow your online business - from how to pick the right suppliers, to proven marketing and SEO strategies, and everything in between. I highly recommend this guide for first-time entrepreneurs and online store owners alike."

—**Shawn Graham,** Marketing Consultant, Shawngraham.me

# The
# *Ultimate Guide*
## to
# DROPSHIPPING

ANDREW YOUDERIAN & MARK HAYES

ISBN: 978-1-4834-0182-9 (sc)

ISBN: 978-1-4834-0181-2 (e)

Lulu Publishing Services rev. date: 06/17/2013

# Contents

# About The Authors

ANDREW YOUDERIAN: Always
the entrepreneur, Andrew sold bootleg
candy as a kid and ran the conventional
lawn business through high school.
In college, he studied finance and
managed to get into trouble with
school officials when he started—and
aggressively marketed—a textbook
exchange business that loudly
denounced the business practices of
the university-owned bookstore.

After a few years of post-college investment banking, he quit to the
dismay of his parents to start his first dropshipping business selling
radio equipment with a $1,500 investment. Since then, he has founded
numerous online stores that collectively generate over $1 million in annual
sales and are run largely by his incredible team in the US and abroad.

With operations in good hands, he took a seven-month sabbatical in 2011 to travel to over 20 countries with his adventurous wife.

Andrew blogs regularly at eCommerceFuel.com where he talks about building ecommerce businesses with an emphasis on helping individual entrepreneurs and smaller niche stores. He's also the author of *Profitable Ecommerce* a detailed guide to picking a dropshipping niche. Andrew currently lives in Bozeman, MT, with his wife Annie and new daughter Claire.

 **MARK HAYES:** Coming from a background in journalism, Mark is an acclaimed writer who has written for some of the top publications in Canada. Mark was a political and cultural commentator at Ottawa Life Magazine, a food and restaurant writer for multiple national magazines, and he has written hundreds of feature articles for Urban Male Magazine, Canada's largest and longest running men's magazine.

In 2010, Mark moved away from journalism and joined the marketing and growth department at Shopify—an ecommerce platform that allows individuals and businesses to easily create beautiful online stores.

Mark is an expert in marketing, communications, social media, public and media relations, content marketing, advertising, and ecommerce.

Mark currently lives in Toronto, Canada. He enjoys restoring and repairing pinball machines, trying new hot sauces, travelling and drinking coffee.

# Introduction

It's DAY THREE OF your week-long mountain biking trip in Utah and you awake to sun streaming through the tent. As the sleepiness fades, you grab your smartphone to check in on your business. The daily report prepared by your virtual assistant is positive: sales were strong yesterday and there were no problems with orders or fulfillment. Smiling, you emerge from your tent to prepare for yet another day of world-class biking as your ecommerce business operates smoothly in the background.

Despite its appeal, you are likely thinking of the difficulty and cost involved with creating such a business. You would need to invest in a warehouse and purchase inventory to sell. Plus, there would be the expense of employees for automating such an operation. Ultimately, the hassle and large investment would make such a business difficult for many people to achieve.

But what if we told you that you could create a business like this without investing a dime in inventory, warehouses or employees. A business with the potential to replace your full-time income and be structured to run on near autopilot for months at a time. Sounds impossible? It's not. The story above—one taken from our own personal experience—is possible with dropshipping.

Dropshipping is a unique retail model that allows you to sell products that others purchase, warehouse and ship for you. In contrast to traditional retailing which requires significant up-front investments, you can leverage dropshipping to start a business with very little money, usually less than $1,000. The model can be used to create a complimentary income stream in addition to your job—or replace it entirely—depending on how much time, effort and work you are willing to put in.

While dropshipping is very attractive, it is by no means a fool proof or "easy" way to make money. The dropshipping model involves some logistical complexities traditional merchants don't have to worry about. It's also an area of ecommerce that's full of "get rich quick" systems and unscrupulous suppliers. With so many rumors and so much misinformation floating around, it's hard to know what to believe—which is exactly why we wrote this guide.

This is the most detailed and thorough guide to dropshipping you will find anywhere. No scams, sales pitches or affiliate links—just the honest truth, written by folks who have used dropshipping to create successful businesses. We won't be telling you what we think might work; we will tell you what we know will work based on our real-world experience.

This guide will teach you everything you need to know to get your own business off the ground while avoiding the costly mistakes that can kill new dropshipping ventures. We will discuss everything from the dropshipping fundamentals to how to operate a dropshipping business and deal with the problems that arise.

Now that you are ready to learn the truth about dropshipping—and how to use it effectively—let's dive in.

## CHAPTER 1

# Understanding Dropshipping

DROPSHIPPING IS A RETAIL fulfillment method where a store does not keep the products it sells in stock. Instead, when a store sells a product, it purchases the item from a third party and has it shipped directly to the customer. As a result, the merchant never sees or handles the product.

The biggest difference between dropshipping and the standard retail model is that the selling merchant does not stock or own inventory. Instead, the merchant purchases inventory as needed from a third party— usually a wholesaler or manufacturer—to fulfill orders.

This unique model has a number of benefits and drawbacks:

## Benefits

**Less Capital Is Required**—Probably the biggest advantage to dropshipping is that it's possible to launch an ecommerce store without having to invest thousands of dollars in inventory up front. Traditionally, retailers have had to tie up huge amounts of capital purchasing inventory.

With the dropshipping model, you don't have to purchase a product unless you already made the sale and have been paid by the customer. Without major up-front inventory investments, it's possible to start a successful dropshipping business with very little money.

**Easy to Get Started**—Running an ecommerce business is much easier when you don't have to deal with physical products. With dropshipping, you don't have to worry about:

- Managing or paying for a warehouse
- Packing and shipping your orders
- Tracking inventory for accounting reasons
- Handling returns and inbound shipments
- Continually ordering products and managing stock level

**Low Overhead**—Because you don't have to deal with purchasing inventory or managing a warehouse, your overhead expenses are quite low. In fact, many successful dropshipping businesses are run from a home office with a laptop for less than $100 per month. As you grow, these expenses will likely increase but will still be low compared to those of traditional brick-and-mortar businesses.

**Flexible Location**—A dropshipping business can be run from just about anywhere with an Internet connection. As long as you can communicate with suppliers and customers easily, you can run and manage your business.

**Wide Selection of Products**—Because you don't have to pre-purchase the items you sell, you can offer an array of products to your potential customers. If suppliers stock an item, you can list if for sale on your website at no additional cost.

**Easy to Scale**—With a traditional business, if you receive three times as much business you will usually need to do three times as much work. By leveraging dropshipping suppliers, most of the work to process additional orders will be borne by the suppliers, allowing you to expand with fewer growing pains and less incremental work. Sales growth will always bring additional work—especially related to customer service—but business that utilize dropshipping scale particularly well relative to traditional ecommerce businesses.

All these benefits make dropshipping a very attractive model to both beginning and established merchants. Unfortunately, dropshipping isn't all roses and rainbows. All this convenience and flexibility comes at a price.

## Disadvantages

**Low Margins**—Low margins are the biggest disadvantage to operating in a highly competitive dropshipping niche. Because it's so easy to get started—and the overhead costs are so minimal—many merchants will set up shop and sell items at rock-bottom prices in an attempt to grow revenue. They've invested so little in getting the business started so they can afford to operate on minuscule margins.

True, these merchants often have low-quality websites and poor (if any) customer service. But that won't stop customers from comparing their prices to yours. This increase in cutthroat competition will quickly destroy the profit margin in a niche. Fortunately, you can do a lot to mitigate this problem by selecting a niche that's well suited for dropshipping. We'll discuss this more in Chapter 4.

**Inventory Issues**—If you stock all your own items, it's relatively simple to keep track of which items are in and out of stock. But when you are sourcing from multiple warehouses, which are also fulfilling orders for other merchants, inventory changes on a daily basis. While there are ways you can better sync your store's inventory with your suppliers', these solutions don't always work seamlessly, and suppliers don't always support the technology required.

**Shipping Complexities**—If you work with multiple suppliers—as most dropshippers do—the products on your website will be sourced through a number of different dropshippers. This complicates your shipping costs.

Let's say a customer places an order for three items, all of which are available only from separate suppliers. You will incur three separate shipping charges for sending each item to the customer, but it's probably not wise to pass this charge along to the customer, as they'll think you are grossly overcharging for shipping. And even if you did want to pass these charges along, automating these calculations can be difficult.

**Supplier Errors**—Have you ever been blamed for something that wasn't your fault, but you had to accept responsibility for the mistake anyway?

Even the best dropshipping suppliers make mistakes fulfilling orders—mistakes for which you have to take responsibility and apologize. And mediocre and low-quality suppliers will cause endless frustration with missing items, botched shipments and low-quality packing, which can damage your business's reputation.

## Is It Worth It?

As we initially warned, dropshipping isn't a perfect, stress-free way to build a successful business. The model has some definite advantages but comes with a number of built-in complexities and problems you will need to be able to address.

We will be examining these problems—and how to best address them—in future chapters. The good news is that with some careful planning and consideration, most of these problems can be resolved and need not prevent you from building a thriving, profitable dropshipping business.

## CHAPTER 2

# The Supply Chain and Fulfillment Process

SUPPLY CHAIN IS A fancy term describing the path a product takes to go from conception through manufacturing and finally into the hands of a customer. If we were talking with hard-core supplier chain gurus, they would insist a product's supply chain reaches all the way to the mining of the materials (like oil and rubber) used to manufacture an item.

For the purposes of this guide, we don't need to get quite that detailed. You simply need to understand the three most applicable players that make up the dropshipping supply chain: manufacturers, wholesalers and retailers.

**Manufacturers**—Manufacturers create the product and most do not sell directly to the public. Instead, they sell in bulk to wholesalers and retailers.

Buying directly from the manufacturer is the cheapest way to purchase products for resale, but most have minimum purchase requirements you will need to meet. You will also need to stock and then re-ship the products when selling them to customers. For these reasons, it's often easier to buy directly from a wholesaler.

**Wholesalers**—Wholesalers buy products in bulk from manufacturers, mark them up slightly and then sell them to retailers for resale to the public. If they do have purchasing minimums, they are generally much lower than those required by a manufacturer.

Wholesalers will usually stock products from dozens—if not hundreds—of manufacturers and tend to operate in a specific industry or niche. Most are strictly wholesaler operators, meaning they sell only to retailers and not directly to the general public.

**Retailers**—A retailer is anyone who sells products directly to the public at a markup. If you run a business that fulfills your orders via dropshipping suppliers, you are a retailer.

## Dropshipping is a Service, Not a Role

You will notice that "dropshipper" is not one of the players listed in the supply chain. Why? Because any of the three—manufacturer, wholesaler or retailer—can act as a dropshipper.

If a manufacturer is willing to ship its products directly to your customer, it is "dropshipping" on your behalf. Similarly, a retail merchant can offer to dropship, although its pricing won't be as competitive as a wholesaler's because it isn't buying directly from the manufacturer.

Just because someone claims to be a "dropshipper" does not mean you are getting wholesale pricing. It simply means the company will ship products on your behalf. To get the best pricing, you want to make sure you are working directly with a legitimate wholesaler or manufacturer, a topic we will be covering in-depth in the next chapter.

## Dropshipping in Action: The Order Process

Now that you understand the players involved, let's take a look at how a dropshipped order gets processed. To illustrate, we'll follow an order placed with our theoretical store, **Phone Outlet**, an online merchant that specializes in accessories for smart phones. Phone Outlet dropships all of its products directly from a wholesaler we will call Wholesale Accessories.

Here's a sample of how the entire ordering process might look:

### Step 1—Customer Places Order With Phone Outlet

Mr. Allen needs a case for his new smartphone and places an order via Phone Outlet's online store. Once the order is approved, a few things happen:

- Phone Outlet and Mr. Allen get an email confirmation (likely identical) of the new order that is automatically generated by the store software.
- Mr. Allen's payment is captured during the checkout process and will be automatically deposited into Phone Outlet's bank account.

## Step 2—Phone Accessory Outlet Places the Order With Its Supplier

This step is usually as simple as Phone Outlet forwarding the email order confirmation to a sales representative at Wholesale Accessories. Wholesale Accessories has Phone Outlet's credit card on file and will bill it for the wholesale price of the goods, including any shipping or processing fees.

> *Note: Some sophisticated dropshippers will support automatic XML (a common format for inventory files) order uploading or the ability to place the order manually online, but email is the most common way to place orders with dropshipping suppliers because it's universal and easy to use.*

## Step 3—Wholesale Accessories Ships the Order

Assuming the item is in stock and the wholesaler was able to successfully charge Phone Outlet's card, Wholesale Accessories will box up the order and ship it directly to the customer. Though the shipment comes from Wholesale Accessories, Phone Outlet's name and address will appear on the return address label and its logo will appear on the invoice and packing slip. Once the shipment has been finalized, Wholesale Accessories will email an invoice and a tracking number to Phone Outlet.

> *Note: The turnaround time on dropshipped orders is often faster than you'd think. Most quality suppliers will be able to get an order out the door in a few hours, allowing merchants to advertise same-day shipping even when they are using a dropshipping supplier.*

## Step 4—Phone Outlet Alerts the Customer of Shipment

Once the tracking number is received, Phone Outlet will send the tracking information to the customer, likely using an email interface that's built in to the online store interface. With the order shipped, the payment collected and the customer notified, the order and fulfillment process is complete. Phone Outlet's profit (or loss) is the difference between what it charged Mr. Allen and what it paid Wholesale Accessories.

## Dropshippers Are Invisible

Despite its critical role in the ordering and fulfillment process, the dropshipper is completely invisible to the end customer. When the package is received, only Phone Outlet's return address and logo will be on the shipment. If Mr. Allen's receives the wrong case, he would contact Phone Outlet, which would then coordinate behind the scenes with Wholesale Accessories to get the right item sent out.

The dropshipping wholesaler doesn't exist to the end customer. Its sole responsibility is to stock and ship products. Everything else—marketing, website development, customer service, etc.—is the responsibility of the merchant.

CHAPTER 3

# Finding and Working With Suppliers

BEFORE SEARCHING FOR SUPPLIERS, it is critical to know how to differentiate between legitimate wholesale suppliers and retail stores posing as wholesale suppliers. A true wholesaler buys directly from the manufacturer and will be able to offer you significantly better pricing.

## How to Spot Fake Dropshipping Wholesalers

Depending on where you are searching, you will likely come across a large number of "fake" wholesalers. Unfortunately legitimate wholesalers are traditionally poor at marketing and tend to be harder to find. This results in the non-genuine wholesalers—usually just middle men—can appear more frequently in your searches so you will want to be cautious and discriminating.

The following tactics will help you discern whether a wholesale supplier is legitimate:

**They Want Ongoing Fees**—Real wholesalers do not charge their customers a monthly fee for the privilege of doing business and ordering from them. If a supplier asks for a monthly membership or service fee, it's likely not legitimate.

It's important to differentiate here between suppliers and supplier directories. Supplier directories (which we will discuss shortly) are directories of wholesale suppliers organized by product types or market and screened to ensure the suppliers are legitimate. Most directories will charge a fee—either onetime or ongoing—so you should not take this as a sign the directory itself is illegitimate.

**They Sell to the Public**—To get genuine wholesale pricing you will need to apply for a wholesale account, prove you are a legitimate business and be approved before placing your first order. Any wholesale supplier that offers products to the general public at "wholesale prices" is just a retailer offering items at inflated prices.

With those in mind, there are a few legitimate wholesale and dropshipping fees you should know about:

**Per-Order Fees**—Many dropshippers will charge a per-order dropshipping fee that can range from $2 to $5 or more, depending on the size and complexity of the items being shipped. This is standard in the industry, as the costs of packing and shipping individual orders are much higher than shipping a bulk order.

**Minimum Order Sizes**—Some wholesalers will have a minimum initial order size, which is the lowest amount you have to purchase for your first order. They do this in order to filter out window-shopping merchants that will waste their time with questions and small orders but won't translate into meaningful business.

If you are dropshipping, this could cause some complications. For example, what do you do if a supplier has a $500 minimum order, but your average order size is around $100? You don't want to pre-order $500 of product just for the privilege of opening a dropshipping account.

In this situation, it's best to offer to pre-pay the supplier $500 to build a credit with them to apply against your dropshipping orders. This allows you to meet the supplier's minimum purchase requirement (as you are committing to buy at least $500 in product) without having to place a single large order without any corresponding customer orders.

# Finding Wholesale Suppliers

Now that you can spot a fraud from the real deal, it's time to start searching for suppliers. You can use a number of different strategies, some more effective than others. The methods below are listed in order of effectiveness and preference, with our favorite methods listed first:

## Contact the Manufacturer

This is our favorite way to easily locate legitimate wholesale suppliers. If you know the product(s) you want to sell, call the manufacturer and ask for a list of its wholesale distributors. You can then contact these wholesalers to see if they dropship and inquire about setting up an account.

Since most wholesalers carry products from a variety of manufacturers, this strategy will allow you to quickly source a selection of products within the niche you are exploring. After making a couple of calls to the leading manufacturers in a niche, you will quickly be able to identify the leading wholesalers in that market.

## Search Using Google

Using Google to find high-quality suppliers may seem obvious, but there are a few rules to keep in mind:

1. **You Have to Search Extensively**—Wholesalers are terrible at marketing and promotion, and they're definitely not going to top the search results for "wholesale suppliers for product X." This means you will likely have to dig through LOTS of search results—possibly hundreds—to find the wholesaler's website listed way down at #65.

2. **Don't Judge by the Website**—Wholesalers are also notorious for having poorly designed '90s-style websites. So while a quality site may indicate a good supplier in some cases, many legitimate wholesalers have cringe-worthy homepages. Don't let the poor design scare you off.

3. **Use Lots of Modifiers**—Wholesalers aren't doing extensive SEO to ensure you find their websites, so you might need to try various search queries. Don't stop at just "[product] wholesaler." Try using modifiers such as "distributor," "reseller," "bulk," "warehouse" and "supplier."

## Order From the Competition

If you are having a hard time locating a supplier, you can always use the old order-from-the-competition trick. Here is how it works: Find a competitor you think is dropshipping and place a small order with that company. When you receive the package, Google the return address to find out who the original shipper was. In some cases, it will be a supplier you can contact.

If you haven't been able to find a supplier using the other techniques discussed above, there might be a good reason (i.e., the market is too small, there's not enough demand to justify a supplier, etc.). So keep this technique in mind, but don't rely too heavily on it.

## Attend a Trade Show

A trade show allows you to connect with all the major manufacturers and wholesalers in a niche. It's a great way to make contacts and research your products and suppliers all in one spot. This only works if you have already selected your niche and/or product, and it isn't feasible for everyone. But if you have the time and money to attend, it's a great way to get to know the manufactures and suppliers in a market.

## Directories

One of the most common questions aspiring ecommerce entrepreneurs ask is: *Should I pay for a supplier directory?*

A supplier directory is a database of suppliers that is organized by market, niche or product. Many directories employ some sort of screening process to ensure the suppliers listed are genuine wholesalers. Most are run by for-profit companies who charge a fee for access to their directory.

While membership directories can be helpful, especially for brainstorming ideas, they are by no means necessary. If you already know the product or niche you want to sell, you should be able to find the major suppliers in your market with a bit of digging and the techniques discussed above. Plus, once you start your business you likely won't need to revisit the directory unless you need to find suppliers for other products.

That said, supplier directories are a convenient way to quickly search for and/or browse a large number of suppliers in one place and are great for brainstorming ideas for products to sell or niches to enter. If you are short on time and are willing to spend the money, they can be a helpful tool.

There are a number of different supplier directories, and a comprehensive review of all of them is beyond the scope of this guide. Instead, we have highlighted some of the most well-known supplier directories online:

## Worldwide Brands

Quick Stats:

- Established: 1999
- Number of suppliers and products: thousands/millions
- Price: $299 for a lifetime membership

Worldwide Brands is one of the oldest and best-known supplier directories. It advertises that it only includes suppliers that meet a set of guidelines to ensure legitimate, quality wholesalers. Membership includes access to dropshipping training and educational content, but this isn't the focus of Worldwide Brand's value. It also has a market research tool that evaluates potential markets and provides a numerical percent chance of success.

We have used the directory in the past to find legitimate wholesalers and to brainstorm niche ideas—and found it useful. Though the directory is missing some suppliers we have worked with, it does include a large collection of legitimate wholesalers. If you want lifetime access to a quality directory and are comfortable with a larger one-time payment, Worldwide Brands is a safe bet.

## SaleHoo

Quick Stats:

- Established: 2005

- Number of suppliers and products: 8,000/NA

- Price: $67 per year

The SaleHoo supplier directory lists more than 8,000 bulk-purchase and dropshipping suppliers, and seems to cater heavily to merchants on eBay, Amazon and other third-party sites. Membership offers access to eBay-specific sales training, a user forum and market research software to help determine what products will sell best.

SaleHoo's $67 annual price is one of the most compelling values among supplier directories and includes a 60-day money-back guarantee. If you are comfortable paying an annual membership—or only need to use a directory temporarily—SaleHoo is worth a look.

## DOBA

Quick Stats:

- Established: 2002

- Number of suppliers and products: 165/1.4 million

- Price: $60 per month

Instead of simply listing suppliers, DOBA's service integrates with dropshippers allowing you to place orders with multiple warehouses using its centralized interface. Membership also includes a Push-to-Marketplace tool that automates the process of listing items on eBay, as well as access to a library of training materials.

DOBA's centralized system offers more convenience then the other directories which is why we imagine the $60 / month fee is higher than other prices. If you place a high value on convenience and can find the products you want among their suppliers, DOBA's interface may be worth the cost.

## WholesaleCentral.com

Quick Stats:

- Established: 1996

- Number of suppliers and products: 1,400 / 740,000

- Price: free

Unlike many other directories, there is no charge to search Wholesale Central for suppliers because it charges suppliers a fee to be listed and also displays ads on their site. They also claim to review and screen all suppliers to ensure they are legitimate and trustworthy.

It's difficult to argue with free, and there's no harm in browsing the listings at WholesaleCentral.com, but you will need to be a bit more discriminating. A number of the suppliers we found appeared to be retailers selling to the public at "wholesale" prices—not something a supplier would do when offering real wholesale pricing. So while we're sure there are genuine wholesale opportunities listed, you may want to be a little more thorough with your due diligence.

## Other Directories

Here are a few other supplier directories you can check out:

- Dropship Design
- DropShippers.com
- Wholesale2b
- Shopster
- Inventory Source
- Sunrise Wholesale Merchandise
- Product Sourcing
- Megagoods
- GoGo Dropship

# Before Contacting Suppliers

Alright, by now we hope you have found a number of solid suppliers and are ready to move forward—great. But before you start contacting companies, you will want to have all your ducks in a row.

**You Need to Be Legal**—As we mentioned earlier, many legitimate wholesalers will require proof that you are a legal business before allowing you to apply for an account. Most wholesalers only reveal their pricing to approved customers, so you will need to be legally incorporated before you will get to see the kind of pricing you will receive.

Bottom line? Make sure you are legally incorporated before contacting suppliers. If you are only looking to ask a few basic questions ("Do you dropship?" "Do you carry brand X?"), you won't need to provide any documentation. But don't expect to launch without having your business properly set up. We will further discuss setting up your business in Chapter 5.

**Understand How You Appear**—Wholesalers are constantly bombarded by people with "great business plans" who pepper them with questions, take up a lot time and then never order anything. So if you are launching a new business, be aware that many suppliers are not going to go out of their way to help you get started.

Most will be happy to set you up with a dropshipping account if they offer it. But don't ask for discount pricing or spend hours tying up their sales representatives on the phone before you have made a single sale. It will quickly earn you a bad reputation and hurt your relationship with the supplier.

If you do need to make special requests (say, trying to convince a supplier to dropship when it normally doesn't), you need to build credibility. Be definitive about your business plans ("We ARE launching this site on January 20) instead of using flaky rhetoric ("I'm thinking about maybe launching a business sometime soon"). And be sure to communicate any professional successes you have had in the past—especially with sales and marketing—that will help you with your new venture.

You need to convince suppliers that the inconvenience of accommodating your special request(s) will pay off down the road when you become successful and start bringing them a ton of business.

**Don't Be Afraid of the Phone**—One of the biggest fears people have when it comes to suppliers is simply picking up the phone and making the call. For many, this is a paralyzing prospect. You might be able to send emails for some issues, but more often than not you will need to pick up the phone to get the information you need.

The good news is that it's not as scary as you might think. Suppliers are accustomed to having people call them, including newbie entrepreneurs. You are likely to get someone who's friendly and more than happy to answer your questions. Here's a tip that will help you, simply write out your questions ahead of time. It's amazing how much easier it is to make the call when you've got a list of pre-written questions to ask.

## How to Find Good Suppliers

Like most things in life, suppliers are not all created equally. In the world of dropshipping—where the supplier is such a critical part of your fulfillment process—it's even more important to make sure you are working with top-notch players.

Great suppliers tend to have many of the following attributes:

**Expert Staff and Industry Focus**—Top-notch suppliers have knowledgeable sales representatives who really know the industry and their product lines. Being able to call a representative with questions is invaluable, especially if you are launching a store in a niche you are not overly familiar with.

**Dedicated Support Representatives**—Quality dropshippers should assign you an individual sales representative responsible for taking care of you and any issues you have. We have dealt with wholesalers that don't assign specific representatives and we hate it. Problems take a lot longer to resolve, and we usually have to nag people to take care of an issue.

Having a single supplier contact that's responsible for solving your issues is really important.

**Invested in Technology**—While there are plenty of good suppliers with outdated websites, a supplier that understands the benefits of—and invests heavily in—technology is usually a pleasure to work with. Features such as real-time inventory, a comprehensive online catalog, customizable data feeds and an online searchable order history are pure luxury for online merchants and can help you streamline your operations.

**Can Take Orders via Email**—This may sound like a minor issue, but having to call every order in—or manually place it on the website—makes processing orders significantly more time-intensive.

**Centrally Located**—If you are in a large country like the United States, it's beneficial to use a centrally located dropshipper, as packages can reach more than 90% of the country within 2 to 3 business days. When a supplier is located on one of the coasts, it can take more than a week for orders to be shipped across the country. Centrally located suppliers allow you to consistently promise faster delivery times, potentially saving you money on shipping fees.

**Organized and Efficient**—Some suppliers have competent staff and great systems that result in efficient and mostly error-free fulfillment. Others will botch every fourth order and make you want to tear your hair out. The trouble is, it's difficult to know how competent a supplier is without actually using it.

Although it won't give you a complete picture, placing a few small test orders can give you a great sense of how a supplier operates. You can see:

1. How they handle the order process

2. How quickly the items ship out

3. How rapidly they follow up with tracking information and an invoice

4. The quality of the pack job when the item arrives

# Your Options on Paying Suppliers

The vast majority of suppliers will accept payment in one of two ways:

## Credit Card

When you are starting out, most suppliers will require you to pay by credit card. Once you have established a thriving business, paying with credit cards is often still the best option. They are not only convenient (no need to write checks regularly), but you can rack up a lot of rewards points/frequent flier miles. Because you are buying a product for a customer who has already paid for it on your website, you can rack up a high volume of purchases through your credit card without having to incur any actual out-of-pocket expenses.

## Net Terms

The other common way to pay suppliers is with "net terms" on invoice. This simply means that you have a certain number of days to pay the supplier for the goods you've purchased. So if you are on "net 30" terms, you have 30 days from the date of purchase to pay your supplier—by check or bank draw—for the goods you bought.

Usually, a supplier will make you provide credit references before offering net payment terms because it's effectively lending you money. This is a common practice, so don't be alarmed if you have to provide some documentation when paying on net terms.

## CHAPTER 4

# Picking Products

THE BIGGEST HURDLE MOST new dropshipping entrepreneurs face is picking a niche and products to focus on. And it's understandable—it's likely the biggest decision you will make and has long-term consequences on the success or failure of the business.

The most common mistake at this stage is picking a product based on personal interest or passion. This is an acceptable strategy if being interested in the product is your primary objective, not necessarily business success. But if your #1 goal is to build a profitable dropshipping site, you will want to consider setting your personal passions aside when doing market research, or at least making sure they meet with the criteria discussed below.

# How to be Successful Selling Online

To build a successful ecommerce business, you will need to do one of the following:

**Manufacture Your Own Product**—You control distribution and are the sole source for the item. This limits competition and allows you to charge a premium price. If you intend to dropship products, you will be selling existing products manufactured by someone else, so this isn't an option.

**Have Access to Exclusive Pricing or Distribution**—If you can arrange an exclusive agreement to carry a product—or if you have access to exclusive pricing from a manufacturer—you can profitably sell online without creating your own product. These arrangements are difficult to arrange, however, and hundreds of other dropship merchants will have access to similar goods and wholesale prices.

**Sell at the Lowest Price**—If you can offer the lowest price, you will likely steal business from a large chunk of the market. The only problem? It's a business model doomed to failure. If the only thing of value you have to offer is a low price, you will be caught in a pricing war that will strip virtually all your profits. Trying to compete against Amazon and other established online giants on price is generally a poor strategy.

**Add Value in Non-Pricing Terms**—Offering valuable information that complements your products is the best way to differentiate yourself and charge a premium price. Entrepreneurs set out to solve people's problems, and that's no different in the world of ecommerce and dropshipping.

Offering expert advice and guidance within your niche is the best way to build a profitable dropshipping business.

**Adding Value in Ecommerce**—Just add value. Simple enough, right? Well, that's easier said than done. Some products and niches lend themselves to this strategy more than others. You should look for a few key characteristics that make adding value with educational content much easier. Specially, you will want to look for niches that:

**Have Many Components**—The more components a product needs to function properly, the more likely customers are to turn to the Internet for answers. Which purchase is more confusing: buying a new office chair or buying a home security camera system that requires multiple cameras, complex wiring and a recorder?

The more components a product needs—and the more variety among those components—the greater your opportunity to add value by advising customers on which products are compatible.

**Are Customizable/Confusing**—Along the same vein, confusing and customizable products are perfect for adding value through content. Would you inherently know how to select the best hot water solar panel configuration for your climate or which type of wireless dog collar system is right for your yard? Being able to offer specific guidance on what types of products are best suited for specific environments and customers is a great way to add value.

**Require Technical Setup or Installation**—It's easy to offer expert guidance for products that are difficult to set up, install or assemble. Take the security camera system from before. Let's say the camera site had a detailed 50-page installation guide that also covered the most common mistakes people make installing their own systems. If you thought the guide could save you time and hassle, there is a good chance you'd buy it from that website even if it was available for a few dollars less elsewhere. For store owners, the guides add tremendous value to customers and don't cost anything to provide once they are created.

## Ways to Add Value:

You can add value to complex and confusing niches in a number of ways, including:

- Creating comprehensive buyers' guides
- Investing in detailed product descriptions and listings
- Creating installation and setup guides (as discussed above)
- Creating in-depth videos showing how the product works
- Establishing an easy-to-follow system for understanding component compatibility

## Cherry-Picking the Best Customers

All customers aren't created equally. It's strange how some customers buying small items feel entitled to demand the moon while other big spenders rarely ask for anything. Targeting the right demographic can be a big boon for your business. These clients tend to make it worth your while:

**Hobbyists**—People love their hobbies and will spend mind-boggling amounts on equipment, training and tools for them. Many serious mountain bikers have bikes that cost more than their cars, and folks who love to fish might spend a fortune outfitting their boats. If you can target the right hobbyist niche and successfully connect with enthusiasts and their needs, you can do very well.

**Businesses**—Business clients are sometimes more price-sensitive but will almost always order in larger quantities than individual consumers. Once you've established a rapport and earned their trust, you open the door to a long-term, high-volume profitable relationship. If at all possible, try to sell products that appeal to both individual customers and businesses.

**Repeat Buyers**—Recurring revenue is a beautiful thing. If you sell products that are disposable and/or need to be reordered frequently, you can grow rapidly as you build a loyal customer base that frequently returns to purchase.

## Other Considerations When Selecting Products

**The Perfect Price**—Make sure you strongly consider the price point relative to the level of pre-sale service you will need to provide. Most people feel comfortable placing a $200 order online without talking to someone on the phone. But what about a $1,500 item they're unfamiliar with? Chances are, most would want to chat directly with a sales representative before making such a large purchase, both to ensure the item is a good fit and to make sure the store is legitimate.

If you plan to sell high-priced items, make sure you are able to offer personalized phone support. You will also want to ensure that the margins are rich enough to justify the pre-sale support you will need to offer. Often, the $50 to $200 price range is the sweet spot to maximize revenue without having to provide extensive pre-sale support.

**MAP Pricing**—Some manufacturers will set what's called a minimum advertised price (MAP) for their products, and require that all resellers price their products at or above certain levels. This pricing floor prevents the price wars that often break out—especially for products that are easily dropshipped—and helps ensure that merchants can make a reasonable profit by carrying a manufacturer's products.

If you can find a niche where manufacturers enforce MAP pricing it's a huge benefit, especially if you plan on building a high-value and information-rich site. With prices the same across all competitors, you can compete on the strength of your website and won't have to worry about losing business to less reputable but cheaper competition.

**Marketing Potential**—The time to think about how you will market a business is before you launch it, not three months in when you realize that customer acquisition is a nightmare. Can you brainstorm a number of ways you could promote your store by, for example, writing articles, giving away products or reaching out to active online communities that use the products you are selling? If not, you may want to reconsider.

**Lots of Accessories**—As a general rule of retail, margins on lower priced accessories are significantly higher than those of high-priced items. While a cell phone store may only make a 5% margin on the latest smartphone, they'll almost certainly make a 100% or 200% margin on the case that goes with it.

As customers, we are much more sensitive about the price on a big-ticket item and care less about the price of smaller accessories. To use the previous example, you would likely shop around for the best price on an expensive smartphone. But are you going to call around to find the best price on a $20 to $30 case? Probably not. You will likely purchase it from the same store where you bought the phone.

Selling a product with many accessories is a great way to improve your overall margin.

**Low Turnover**—We hope you are convinced by now that investing in an education-rich, high-quality site will pay big dividends. But if the products you sell change every year, maintaining that site is quickly going to turn into a mountain of work. Try to find products that aren't updated with new models every year. That way, the time and money you invest in a superb site will last longer.

**Hard to Find Locally**—Selling a product that is difficult to find locally will increase your chances of success as long as you don't get too specific. Most people needing a garden rake or a sprinkler would simply run down to the local hardware store. But where would you buy a medieval knight's costume or falcon training equipment? You'd probably head to Google and start searching.

**Smaller Is Usually Better**—In a world where free shipping is often expected, it can be a challenge to sell large, heavy equipment that's expensive to ship. The smaller the items, the easier they are to ship cheaply to your customers.

Picking a profitable niche isn't easy and requires you to consider numerous factors. These guidelines should give you a good idea of the types of dropshipped products that work well.

## Measuring Demand

Without demand, it doesn't matter if your niche fits 100% of the attributes listed above. If nobody wants your product, you will have a hard time making any money. As the old saying goes, it's much easier to fill existing demand than to try to create it.

Fortunately, a number of online tools allow you to measure demand for a product or market. The most well-known and popular is the Google Keyword Tool.

# Google Keyword Tool

The best way to measure demand for an item online is to see how many people are searching for it using a search engine like Google. Fortunately, Google makes this search volume publicly available via its keyword tool. Simply type in a word or phrase, and the tool tells you how many people are searching for it every month.

There are entire training modules dedicated to using the keyword tool, and we're not able to cover the tool exhaustively in this book. But keep the following three tips in mind, and you will be well on your way to getting the most out of the tool:

**Match Type**—The tool will let you select broad, phrase or exact match types when it reports search volumes. Unless you have a good reason to do otherwise, you should use the exact match option. This will give you a much more accurate picture of the applicable search volume for the keyword. For a more detailed explanation, see this article on understanding match types.

**Search Location**—Make sure you look at the difference between local search volume (in your country or a user-defined region) and global search volumes. If you will be selling primarily in the U.S., you should focus on the local search volumes and ignore the global results, as that is where most of your customers will be.

**Long-Tail Variations**—It's easy to fixate on the broad, one- or two-word search terms that get massive amounts of search volume. In reality, it's the longer, more specific and lower volume search queries that will make up most of your traffic from the search engines. These longer, more detailed search terms are commonly referred to as "long-tail" searches.

Keep this in mind when you are looking at potential markets and niches to enter. If a search term has many variations that are actively searched for, that's a good sign that the market is fairly deep with lots of variety and interest. But if search queries and related volume drop off precipitously after the first few high-level words, there's probably less related long-tail traffic.

## Google Trends

The keyword tool is great for raw search figures, but for more detailed insights you will want to use Google Trends. The tool offers you information that the Keyword Tool just doesn't provide, including:

**Search Volume Over Time**—Ideally, you want the niche you are entering to be growing and Trends can let you know if this is the case. For any given search query, you can see the growth or decline in search volume over time. Below is a chart of search volume for the term "smartphone". As expected, search volume has risen sharply in the last few years:

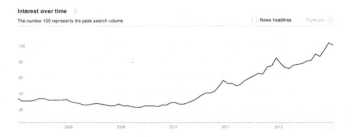

**Top and Rising Terms**—You will also be able to get a snapshot at the most popular related searches, and which queries have been growing in popularity the fastest. Focusing on these popular and quickly growing terms can be helpful when planning your marketing and SEO efforts. According to the charts below, search queries related to AT&T, Verizon and Samsung seem to be experiencing the most growth in the smart phone market—data which shows up when we analyze the term "smartphone":

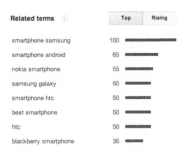

**Geographical Concentration**—Another useful feature is the ability to see where people are searching for a term geographically. This can help you identify where your customer base for a niche is most heavily concentrated. For example, if you are selling canoes the charts below can help you determine that the majority of your customers will likely come from the Northern U.S., Alaska and Hawaii. If you were trying to decide between multiple suppliers, this knowledge could help you partner with one closest to the majority of your customers:

**Seasonality**—Understanding the seasonality of a market—that is, if the demand for a product changes dramatically at different points in the year—is crucially important. Because the keyword tool provides data on a monthly basis, you can draw some misleading conclusions if you measure search volumes during the wrong time of year.

Revisiting our previous example, we can see below that "canoes" are a very seasons search term with demand peaking in the summer months. If you measured demand in the summer expecting that it would be constant throughout the year, you'd grossly overestimate the size of demand:

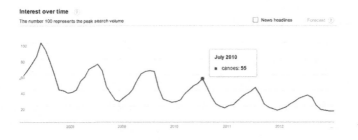

For any product you are seriously considering, you will want to spend time understanding the intricacies of the niche's search volume. Using the Google Trend tool to understand search volumes, geographic concentration, high-level search trends and seasonality will offer insights that can help you avoid costly mistakes and optimize your marketing efforts.

## Measuring Competition

Conducting competitive analysis on a potential market can be tricky. Too much competition and you will have difficulty building traffic and competing with established players. Too little competition can indicate a tiny market that will drastically limit how big you will be able to grow.

Some dropshipping stores use paid advertising, but most will rely heavily on free traffic from the search engines to build a profitable business model. With this in mind, the best way to measure the overall competition in a market is to examine the organically listed (i.e., not advertised) sites on the first page of Google for a specific term. In order to generate a decent level of traffic, you will need to successfully compete with (i.e., outrank) the sites on Google's first page.

The world of search engine optimization (SEO) is one we can't do justice in this article. But for the sake of evaluating competition, these four metrics will help you quickly gauge how strong the field is—and how hard it will be to outrank your competitors and generate traffic.

# Number of Linking Domains

Google's ranking algorithm relies heavily on links. All else equal, the more links a site receives the higher it will rank in the search results. Knowing how many links are pointing to a site will give you an idea of how much work you will need to do (in terms of earning and building links to your own site) to outrank your competitor.

There are dozens of different SEO metrics that are commonly used, but one in particularly is useful when evaluating the ranking strength of a site: the number of unique domains that link to it. Often called "linking root domains" or "unique linking domains", this metric represents the number of unique domains (ie independent sources) that link to a site and ignores duplicate links from the same domain.

To best understand this concept it's helpful to think of links like personal recommendations. If your best friend comes to you and recommends a restaurant, you may remember it. And if he raves about it every day for a week (a total of seven recommendations) you will likely be moved to eat there. But even his fanaticism wouldn't be nearly as powerful as if seven unique, unrelated friends highly recommended the restaurant. Because they're independent sources, their recommendations hold much more authority.

The same is true when analyzing links to a site. A domain can link to a site repeatedly, but it's really one "unique" recommendation, and this is where common SEO metrics like "total number of links" can paint an inaccurate picture when measuring a site's strength. Instead, looking at the number of unique linking domains will give you a much better idea of how difficult it will be to compete with a site in the search results. Google places a high emphasis on unique linking domains, so you should, too.

The best way to get this figure is to use a tool called Open Site Explorer. Developed by a company called SEOMoz, Open Site Explorer provides a number of valuable SEO metrics and data. For full functionality, you will need to purchase a paid membership but it's possible to get the metric we want—"Linking Root Domains" as labeled by the tool—for free.

When examining Google's search results, you will want to look most carefully at the link metrics for the top few sites (#1 and #2 in Google) as well as the link metrics for the last site on the front page (#10 in Google). This will give you a rough idea of how much work is needed to not only rank #1, but also to simply make it on the first page of search results. The vast majority of searchers end up clicking on one of the top ten results in Google, so you want to understand how difficult it will be to get your site ranked there.

Here's a quick cheat sheet for interpreting the number of unique linking domains. (These are only rough guidelines but should help you make sense of the numbers.)

**0 to 50 Linking Root Domains**: Will likely be on the low end for most worthwhile markets. Most sites with quality content and some focused marketing and SEO effort should be able to get 50 linking domains within a year.

**50 to 250 Linking Root Domains**: This is a more realistic range for top-ranked sites in decently sized niche markets. It may take a multi-year approach to build a backlink profile in this range, but it's feasible. A competitive landscape with this profile often offers the best work-to-reward ratio, especially for individual dropshipping entrepreneurs or very small teams.

**250+ Linking Root Domains:** Unless you are a talented marketer or SEO ninja, building up more than 250 unique links will take some serious time and commitment. It's not always a deal killer—just make sure you are ready to face some entrenched competition.

## Authority of Competing Sites

When determining a site's rank, Google doesn't just look at the number of links a site has. It also considers the quality of those links. So a link from Mike's Marshmallow Blog with five readers won't count anywhere close to as much as a link from The New York Times.

The metric Google uses to measure a page's authority is called PageRank. It's not the end-all-be-all of SEO metrics, but it's a quick way to get an idea of how important Google thinks a page is. As with unique linking sites, you can get a sense for how competitive a market is by looking at the PageRank for the homepages of top-ranked sites.

The easiest way to check PageRank is with a browser extension such as SearchStatus for Firefox. You can also check sites manually using sites like this one www.checkpagerank.net.

Here's a quick way to interpret PageRank readings for a site's homepage:

**PageRank 1 to 2:** A relatively small amount of authority. PageRank in this range for the top homepages likely indicates a relatively small market.

**PageRank 3 to 4:** A much more common range for highly ranked sites in competitive niche markets. It's not necessarily easy to reach this level of authority—but not impossible, either. Markets in this range usually offer the best work-to-reward range for individual dropshippers.

**PageRank 4 to 5:** A fairly high level of authority. To reach this level, you will need to get numerous links from respected, authoritative sites, in addition to a fair number of other links.

**PageRank 6+:** You've got a full-time marketing and SEO department, right? Because you will need them to compete in a market with sites like this.

## Qualitative Metrics to Consider

Hard statistics like unique linking domains and PageRank can be helpful in determining how hard it will be to outrank competitors, but it's also very important to look at a few qualitative factors:

**Site Quality and Usefulness**—Visit the top-ranked sites for a market and put yourself in the shoes of a customer. Do they appear inviting and welcoming or old and outdated? Are the sites well-organized and easy to navigate or is it a struggle to even find the search box? Do they provide high-quality information and detailed product listings or do you have to squint to make out the grainy product images?

In short, how likely would you be to purchase from those sites? If you are blown away by the top sites in a market, it will be difficult to differentiate yourself and you may want to consider a different market. But if there's a lot of room for improvement—or, as we see it, opportunity to add value—that's a great sign.

**Site Reputation and Customer Loyalty**—An online business might have a solid reputation based on years of treating customers well, despite a drab design and outdated site. Alternatively, the most beautifully designed site might have a widespread reputation for awful customer service. It can be difficult to judge a book by its cover.

Check with the Better Business Bureau to see if a company has a history of customer complaints. You will also want to do a web search to see what people are saying on social media and in online forums and communities. If the top competitors are slacking in the service and satisfaction department, there might be an opening for a store with superior service.

## An Important Note on Search Results

When you perform a search, it's important to realize that Google personalizes the results you see based on your geographic location, your browsing history and other factors. When we're analyzing a market, we need to see unbiased results so we can understand the real competitive landscape. Also, if you are living outside the states but plan on selling to U.S. customers you need access to the search results your U.S.-based customers will see as those are the sites you will be competing with.

There are two ways to get around these issues:

**Incognito Search**—If you use Chrome as a browser, you can browse the web 'Incognito'. In this mode, any personalized settings or browsing history will discarded so you can get an unbiased idea of how sites actually rank. You can start an Incognito browsing sessions by going to "File— New Incognito Window" or by clicking on the icon in the upper right hand corner of your browser and selecting "New Incognito Window".

**Forcing Nation-Specific Results**—If you would like to see the results that appear for a nation other than your own, you can add a small amount of text to the end of the URL on a Google results page to get country specific results.

For example, if you were in the UK but wanted to see the search results being returned to searches in the US, you'd add the "&gl=us" parameter to the end of the URL on the search results page and press enter. Similarly, if you were in the US and wanted to get UK results you'd add "&gl=uk" to the end of the URL.

## Higher Risk Items to Sell

There are some items that are more difficult to sell online. Either the market is already completely saturated, they are against eBay's listing policies, or many ecommerce platforms do not allow merchants to sell them. Here is a list of some items that are often deemed high risk and will require further investigation to see if they can or should be sold online:

- Adult material

- Alcohol

- Animals (ivory, etc)

- Artifacts

- Catalytic converters (automotive equipment that is illegal)

- Cellular phone contracts

- Coins or currency

- Credit cards

- Drugs

- Embargoed goods (items from Cuba to the US)

- Event tickets

- Firearms

- Gift cards

- Government documents

- Hazardous, restricted, and perishable items
- Human parts
- Items encouraging illegal activity (a book describing how to create a bomb, or drugs)
- Lock picking materials
- Lottery tickets
- Mailing lists
- Medical devices (surgical instruments)
- Pesticides
- Police-related items
- Prescription drugs
- Prohibited services
- Real estate
- Recalled items
- Slot machines
- Stock and other securities
- Stolen property
- Surveillance equipment
- Tobacco
- Travel
- Weeds and seeds

## One Final Thing

Aspiring dropshipping entrepreneurs commonly want to know, *How can I be sure that my niche will work out?* The answer is, you can't. While the tips and guidance in this chapter will dramatically increase your chances and help you make an informed decision, there's no way to know for sure if you will succeed in a market without diving in. We have started numerous businesses—some of which succeeded and some of which flopped—and we have always had doubts at the beginning. That's part of the uncertainty that comes with starting a business and venturing into the unknown. What separates entrepreneurs from mere dreamers is a willingness to move forward despite the uncertainty and give it their best.

So do your homework, research and gather as much information as possible. But then make the best decision you can and move forward despite your hesitations and fears. If you wait for all uncertainties to be resolved with "the perfect market," you will never get started.

# CHAPTER 5

## Starting Your Business

AT THIS POINT, YOU should have the dropshipping fundamentals down and you may be contemplating launching a business. Before you get started, you will want to consider taking the following business and financial steps if you are serious about your new venture. Some are mandatory from the outset while others are just a good idea, but dealing with them up front will save you time and headaches down the road.

## The Commitment Required

As with any other business, building a successful dropshipping business takes significant commitment and a long-term perspective. If you are hoping for a six-figure income from six weeks of part-time work, you are going to be sadly disappointed. By approaching your business with realistic expectations about the investment required and your profitability, you will be much less likely to get discouraged and quit.

When starting a dropshipping business, you will need to invest heavily using one of the following two currencies: time or money.

# Investing Time

Bootstrapping and investing sweat equity to build your business is our recommended approach, especially for first-time dropshipping entrepreneurs. We favor this approach over investing a large sum of money for numerous reasons:

- You will learn how the business operates inside and out, which will be crucial for managing others as your business grows and scales.
- You will intimately know your customers and market, allowing you to make better decisions.
- You will be less likely to spend large sums on vanity projects that aren't critical to success.
- You will develop several new skills that will make you a better entrepreneur.

Realistically, most people aren't able to quit their job to spend six months ramping up their new online store. It may be a bit more challenging, but it's definitely possible to get started with dropshipping even if you are still working a 9-to-5 position assuming you set appropriate expectations regarding customer service and fulfillment times for your customers. As you start to grow, you can then transition into working full-time on your business as cash flow and profitability allows.

All businesses and entrepreneurs are unique, but it is possible to generate a $1,000—$2,000 monthly income stream within 12 months working approximately 10 to 15 hours per week building your business.

If you have the option to work on your business full-time, it is the best choice to improve your profit potential and chance of success. Focusing all your efforts on marketing is especially helpful in the early days when building momentum is crucial. Based on our experience, it will usually take at least 12 months of full-time work with a strong emphasis on marketing for a dropshipping business to replace an average full-time income of $50,000.

It may seem like a lot of effort for a relatively small payoff, but keep these two things in mind:

- Once your dropshipping business is up and running, maintaining it will likely take significantly less time than a 40-hour-per-week job. Much of your investment pays off in terms of the efficiency and scalability offered by the dropshipping model.

- When you build a business, you are creating more than just an income stream—you are also building an asset that you can sell in the future. Make sure you consider the equity value you are accruing as well as the cash flow generated when looking at your true return.

# Investing Money

It is possible to create and grow a dropshipping business by investing a bunch of money, but we advise against it. We have tried both approaches to growing a business (bootstrapping it ourselves versus outsourcing the process) and have had the most success when we have been in the trenches doing most of the work.

In the early stages, it is crucial to have someone who is deeply invested in the success of the business building it from the ground up. Without understanding how your business works at every level, you will be at the mercy of expensive programmers, developers and marketers who will quickly eat up any profits you are generating. You don't need to do absolutely everything yourself, but we strongly recommend being the primary driving force at the outset of your venture.

You will, however, need a small cash cushion in the $1,000 range to get your business launched and operational. You will need this for minor operating expenses (such as web hosting and suppliers) and to pay any incorporation fees, which we'll discuss below.

# Deciding on a Business Structure

If you are serious about your venture, you will want to set up a legitimate business entity. We are not lawyers and cannot offer legal advice but we can give you a rundown of three commonly used business structures:

**Sole Proprietorship**—This is the simplest business structure to implement but also offers no personal liability protection. So if your business is sued, your personal assets also may be in jeopardy. Filing requirements are minimal, and you simply report your business's earnings on your personal taxes. No other state or federal business filings are required.

**Limited Liability Company (LLC)**—An LLC offers increased protection of your personal assets by establishing your business as a separate legal entity. While the liability protection isn't foolproof, it does offer more protection than a sole proprietorship. You may need to comply with additional filing requirements and will need to pay both incorporation and ongoing fees.

**C Corporation**—Most major corporations are set up as C corporations which, when done properly, offer the most liability protection. They are likely to be more expensive to incorporate and are subject to double taxation, as income doesn't pass directly to the shareholders.

So which structure to choose? Again, we're not lawyers and would advise you to consult with one before making any incorporation decisions. Most small entrepreneurs tend to go with either a sole proprietorship or an LLC. Personally, we have used an LLC for all of our dropshipping businesses because we feel it offers the best trade-off regarding liability protection, autonomy from personal finances and costs.

## Requesting an EIN Number

The IRS requires all businesses to have an employer identification number (EIN), which acts as a Social Security number for your business. You will need this number to file your taxes, apply for wholesale dropshipping accounts, open a bank account and pretty much do anything related to your business.

Fortunately, getting an EIN number is easy and free. You can easily apply for an EIN number online at www.irs.gov.

## Getting Your Finances in Order

One common mistake entrepreneurs make when starting a business is blending their personal and business finances. This causes confusion, makes accounting more difficult, can lead to personal assumption of business liabilities and is a big red flag for the IRS if you are ever audited.

You will want to keep your business and personal finances separate as much as possible. The best way to do that is by opening up new accounts in your business's name. You will want to open a new:

**Business Checking Account**—You should run all of your business finances through one primary checking account. All business revenue should be deposited into it and all expenses should be withdrawn from it. This will make accounting much easier and cleaner.

**PayPal Account**—If you plan to accept PayPal (which you likely will), you will want a separate account for your business. Many businesses based in the United States use Stripe payment gateway (www.stripe.com), it is easy to setup and offers reasonable rates.

**Credit Card**—You should have a business credit card that is used for business expenses and dropshipping inventory purchases only. Because you will be buying a lot of merchandise from suppliers, you can rack up some serious rewards with the right rewards travel cards. We have found that Capital One has the best travel rewards program, and that Fidelity Visa/American Express offers the best cash-back program.

## Collecting Sales Tax

> *Disclaimer: While this information is accurate as of publication, there is currently legislation in the U.S. Congress that proposes requiring all*

*online merchants to collect sales tax on a national level. This policy may change in the very near future, so please make sure to look into this when you're preparing to launch your store.*

You will need to collect sales tax only if both the following are true:

- The state you operate from collects sales tax AND
- An order is placed by someone living in your state

For all orders placed by residents of other states—even if those states charge their own sales tax—you won't need to collect any tax. There's a good chance we'll see changes to these laws in the coming years, but for now the tax laws for small online merchants are very advantageous.

If your state does charge sales tax, be prepared to collect it on the limited number of orders from customers in your home state. You will want to contact your state's Department of Commerce to register as a retailer and find out how frequently you need to submit the tax you collect.

## Local Business Licenses

Most cities and towns require businesses to get a business license that needs to be renewed on a regular basis. However, this requirement may differ for dropshipping businesses, many of which will likely be operated from home offices. You will want to look into your local laws and regulations to see what, if anything, is required.

## Incorporating Outside the U.S.

It can be complex, but it's possible for international merchants to incorporate a business in the United States, giving them access to U.S. based dropshippers and customers. The merchant will need to come to the U.S. to complete the necessary paperwork, have a trusted business partner in the U.S. who can act on his behalf or hire an agency to set everything up.

## Chapter 6

# Evaluating Sales Channels

WITH A PRODUCT PICKED, suppliers secured and your business legally established, it's time to start selling. Next, you need to decide how to get your products in front of prospective customers. Several sales options are available, but you will most likely choose one of these three: selling on eBay, Amazon or your own online store.

## Dropshipping on eBay

As the world's largest auction site for physical goods online, eBay is a site most people know well. The following are some reasons you might want to consider—or avoid—dropshipping on eBay:

## The Pros of Selling on eBay

**Easy to Get Started**—With eBay you can immediately dive in and start listing your wholesale products for sale. Create an account, add a listing and you are in business.

**Access to a Large Audience**—When you list on eBay, you have access to the many online buyers who frequent the auction giant. Millions of people will see your listings, and the fairly robust and active market will help ensure you get a decent price for your products.

**No Need to Market**—Because you are able to piggyback off eBay's enormous platform, you don't need to worry about marketing, SEO or paying for traffic. This saves you significant time, as marketing is one of the biggest challenges associated with launching a dropshipping business.

**Easy to Take a Break**—Need some time off from your business? No problem. With eBay auctions, you can simply stop listing products for a short period and enjoy some time off. If you are selling on Amazon or your own online store, this is more difficult to do.

## The Cons of Selling on eBay

**Listing Fees**—The biggest downside to eBay are the fees you will have to pay. The most notable is the success fee, which can be up to 10%—or higher—of the sale prices of your items. In the dropshipping market, where margins are already fairly thin, this will cut into a large portion of your profits.

**Constant Monitoring and Re-Listing**—eBay is an auction-style marketplace, so you will need to be constantly monitoring and re-listing the products you want to sell. Some tools help automate this process, but it's still not as straightforward as listing a static product for sale on your own website.

**Can't Customize Your Sales Platform**—Your product listings need to follow eBay templates, making it more difficult to create a professional, value-adding page for your items.

**No Long-Term Connection With Customers**—You might have a few repeat eBay customers, but most will probably never buy from you again. Any goodwill you bank up through excellent service will likely be lost.

**You are Not Building an Asset**—When you create a store that generates traffic and has repeat customers, you are building a real business with value that you can sell to someone else. When you sell on eBay, you are not building a lasting brand or web property with any tangible value that can be sold in the future.

# Dropshipping on Amazon

Although Amazon stocks and sells a number of items, many of the products listed are actually sold by third-party merchants via Amazon's website. Like eBay, Amazon acts to help facilitate the sale and to resolve any problems that arise.

## The Pros of Selling on Amazon

The advantages of selling on Amazon are similar to the ones discussed for eBay: it's easy to get started, you have immediate access to a large audience and you do not need to worry about marketing or SEO. Amazon also offers its own fulfillment warehouses (Fulfillment by Amazon), which allow you to complement your dropshipped items with products of your own without having to deal with packing, shipping or warehousing.

## The Cons of Selling on Amazon

As with eBay, you pay for access to this large network of buyers through commission fees. Amazon's commission fees vary by product type but are usually in the 10% to 15% range. Again, if you are working with relatively small dropshipping margins, this will take a hefty chunk out of your profits.

When you are selling exclusively on Amazon, like eBay, it's more difficult to build a loyal customer base and a business with real equity.

# Dropshipping With Your Own Store

The alternative to selling through third-party sites like Amazon and eBay is establishing your own storefront to sell products.

## The Pros of Selling on Your Own Store

With your own online store you get to create a shopping environment that is conducive to selling your products and—most importantly—adding value to your customers. You can customize the look and layout, and create custom product pages optimized to best inform your customers about the products.

**More Control**—With your own online store you get to create a shopping environment that's conductive to selling your products and—most importantly—adding value to your customers. You can customize the look and layout, and create custom product pages optimized to best inform your customers about the products.

**Easy Design**—Building your own ecommerce store is easy, especially with platforms like Shopify. Simply choose a store design out of hundreds of options, make any customizations you want, add your products, hook up a payment gateway and you're up and running. Depending on the type of online store you're looking to create, you can be up and running in one day.

**Mobile Ready**—Selling on eBay and Amazon via mobile can be a pain. If you choose to build your online store with well-respected hosted ecommerce platform your site will likely be responsive, which means it will look great on an iPad or mobile phone. This is increasingly important these days, as nearly 30% of online purchases are made via a mobile device.

Some online store platforms, like Shopify, let you manage your entire business from your mobile device. This is particularly attractive to dropshipping business owners who often like to run their business on-the-go, or even on the beach somewhere.

**No Third-Party Fees**—You won't have to pay 10% to 15% of every sale to eBay or Amazon, which will significantly improve your profit margins. All-in-all you're going to make more money by setting your dropshipping business up with an online store.

**Building a Real Business**—You're able to build a long-term business with a distinctive feel, known expertise and repeat customers. Most importantly, you'll be building a business with equity. It's much easier to sell a business built around an independently owned website.

## The Cons of Selling on Your Own Store

**Less Free Traffic**—With your own site, you'll be responsible for generating traffic through marketing, SEO and paid advertising. There's more cost involved—either money or time invested—and you'll need to be willing to invest in a long-term campaign to promote your new store.

**Increased Complexity**—On Amazon and eBay, you don't have to think too much; simply fill out the standard template and publish your product listing. With your own site, you're ultimately responsible for configuring the design, layout and structure of your store. And if you're hosting your own store (versus using a hosted service like Shopify), you'll be responsible for any technical configuration related to the software and servers.

## Which Sales Strategy Should You Choose?

So which platform should you choose? There's a lot to consider, and different platforms will be better suited for different people and situations.

If you're looking to dip your toes into the dropshipping waters and explore it as a hobby, selling on eBay and Amazon can be a viable way to move forward if you can find products with enough margin to cover your fees and still make a profit. There are many people making money selling on eBay and Amazon so you shouldn't dismiss it.

But if you're serious about building a long-term business, we recommend starting your own ecommerce store. As discussed above, it offers the most flexibility, customization, ability to connect with customers, the chance to build real brand equity, and so much more. You'll need to invest in marketing and promotion, especially in the early days, but we think it offers the best long-term potential and is truly the only option for those serious about selling online.

Also, there's nothing wrong with selling a few items on eBay and Amazon while you're in the early stages of building your store. In fact, a number of mature, established brands sell merchandise this way, particularly through Amazon.

If you're interested in starting an online store, we suggest signing up for a 30-day free trial with Shopify. Simply go to www.shopify.com/dropship to learn more.

CHAPTER 7

# Running a Dropshipping Business

IF YOU'VE NEVER RUN a dropshipping business, the information in this chapter could save you weeks of wasted time and frustration. Many of these detailed suggestions are drawn from two basic principles about dropshipping:

1. **Accept That Things Can Get Messy**—The convenience of dropshipping comes at a price, and having an invisible third party involved in each sale often complicates things. From botched orders to out-of-stock items, fulfillment problems will be

something you will have to deal with. If you accept this ahead of time, you are less likely to throw in the towel due to frustration.

2. **Adopt a KISS Mentality**—Having a KISS (Keep It Simple, Stupid) mentality will serve you well with the dropshipping model. Given the inherent complexity of dropshipping—multiple suppliers, shipments from various locations, etc.—it's easy to think you need to set your system to perfectly track your costs and inventory at all times. But if you try to do this, you will likely go crazy, spend thousands on custom development and never launch a store. Focusing on the easiest-to-implement solutions, even if they're not "perfect," is usually the better option—especially when you are starting out.

With these two concepts in mind, let's discuss how to structure your business operationally to make things run as smoothly as possible.

## When Suppliers Botch an Order

Even great suppliers make mistakes, and you are guaranteed to have fulfillment errors from time to time. So what do you do when your supplier sends the wrong item—or nothing at all?

**Own the Mistake**—Under no circumstances should you blame your dropshipper for the mistake. It will only cause confusion and make you look like an amateur. The customer has no idea the dropshipper even exists. Instead, you need to own the problem, apologize and let the customer know what you are doing to fix it.

**Make It Up to Them**—Depending on the level of the mistake, you may want to proactively offer the customer something for the error. This could mean refunding the shipping fee (a personal favorite of ours) or an upgrade if the customer needs a new item shipped out.

**Make the Supplier Pay to Fix It**—You may have to assume responsibility for the error, but that doesn't mean you need to pay for it. Any reputable supplier will pay to fix its own errors, including paying for shipping costs to return items. However, it probably won't pay for any freebies or upgrades you gave the customer. You need to chalk those up as public relations and brand-building expenses.

Again, even the best suppliers will occasionally make mistakes, but be extremely wary of a supplier that habitually botches your orders and fails to fulfill them properly. Unless you can get the supplier to change (unlikely), your business's reputation will suffer. If this is the case, you should probably start looking for another supplier.

## Managing Inventory & Multiple Suppliers

Most experienced dropshippers would agree that managing the status of inventory across multiple suppliers is the biggest challenge you will face running a dropshipping business. Do a poor job of this and you will be constantly informing customers that their order is out of stock—not a great way to attract repeat business and loyal brand fans.

Properly managing inventory across your suppliers—and limiting the number of out-of-stock items you sell—is a complex process. Web-based services, like Ordoro and eCommHub can help you sync inventory. This is a great option when suppliers offer real-time data feeds, but suppliers don't always have them. Below are some best practices for inventory management that should help drastically reduce the number of out-of-stock items you sell:

1. **Use Multiple Suppliers**—Having access to multiple suppliers is so crucial, we wouldn't start a new dropshipping business if we could only source our product line through one location. Why? Because having multiple suppliers with overlapping inventory is

the best way to improve your order fulfillment ratio. If supplier **A** doesn't have an item in stock, there's a good chance supplier **B** has it. Additionally, it's risky to rely on one supplier as the only place to source your product. If they decide not to work with you, raise their prices or go out of business it jeopardizes the future of your business.

You will never be able to find two suppliers that carry all the same products, but if they operate in the same niche or industry, both will likely stock the best-selling items—and these are what you are most concerned about.

2. **Pick Your Products Wisely**—Drawing on the last point, try to sell primarily items that you know are carried by both suppliers. This way, you have two potential fulfillment options.

3. **Use Generics to Your Advantage**—Even if they don't have exactly the same item, two suppliers might carry near-identical products that are interchangeable. This is particularly true for smaller accessories and product add-ons. If you can confirm that two products are nearly identical, write a generic product description that allows you to fulfill the order from either supplier. Also, list both suppliers' model numbers in the model field. That way you can forward an order invoice to either supplier without having to make changes.

A word of warning: You need to exercise some judgment in this area. Each market will have well-known brands (e.g., Nike, Bose), and you should NEVER substitute those products.

4. **Check on Item Availability**—Just because a dropshipper lists an item on its website doesn't mean it carries that item consistently. It's a good idea to chat with your sales representative about the

availability of products you are considering selling. Are these items in stock 90% of the time or more? Or does the dropshipper keep only a few on hand and often has trouble getting the product reordered from the manufacturer? You will want to avoid stocking the latter type of products.

5. **Dealing With Out-of-Stock Orders**—Despite your best planning, you will inevitably deal with customer orders you can't fill. Instead of telling the customer the item is out of stock, offer a complimentary upgrade to a similar—but better— product. Your customer will likely be thrilled, and you will be able to retain the customer relationship. You might not make any money on the order, and that is perfectly fine. You wouldn't have made any money had your customer canceled the order, either.

## Order Fulfillment

Utilizing multiple suppliers has a number of benefits that we have discussed: it increases the likelihood that items will be in stock, offers geographical diversity for faster delivery times and prevents you from being reliant on any one source for your products. But with multiple options for filling an order, how do you know which supplier to choose? There are a few different methods to consider:

**Route All Orders to a Preferred Supplier**—If you have one supplier that is best to work with (superior service, great selection, etc.), you can simply route all orders to that supplier by default. This is particularly easy to implement, as you can simply add your supplier's email address as a recipient for all new order confirmations, automating the entire process. If you use this method, ideally your preferred supplier will stock most of the items you sell. Otherwise, you will frequently have to deal with re-routing orders that it couldn't fill.

**Route Orders Based on Location**—If you use multiple suppliers that each stock the majority of your products, you can simply route the order to the supplier closest to your customer. This not only expedites delivery to your customer, but also saves on shipping fees.

**Route Orders Based on Availability**—If you stock a large catalog of products spread out over numerous suppliers, you will likely need to route each order based on which dropshipper has the item in stock. This option requires more work if you are doing it manually but can be automated with a service like eCommHub or Orodoro if your suppliers provide data feeds.

**Route Orders Based on Price**—This sounds great in theory, but unless one supplier has significantly better pricing it can be difficult to automatically determine which supplier will be cheapest. Any automated solution will need to consider potential drop fees, real-time shipping rates and real-time supplier pricing. So while not impossible, it can be difficult to implement an accurate automated system to accomplish this.

> *Note: Even if you don't route all your orders on price, you should have your suppliers bid against each other to achieve the best pricing possible as your business grows. Just don't try to do this too early—if you are asking for pricing discounts as a newbie, you will likely only annoy your suppliers.*

We have tried all four methods and found there's no "best" way to do it. It really depends on your store, your suppliers and your personal preferences.

# Security and Fraud Issues

## Storing Credit Card Numbers

Storing your customers' credit card information can allow for convenient reordering and may increase sales. But if you are hosting your own site, this typically isn't worth the security issues and liability. To store credit card data you will need to abide by all sorts of PCI (Payment Card Industry) compliance rules and security audits. This process is expensive and complex, especially for non-technical merchants. And if your server is hacked or breached, you might be liable for the stolen card information.

The best solution is to not store your customers' credit card data. Focus your efforts on marketing and customer service instead of security audits. Fortunately, if you are using a hosted platform like Shopify you won't need to worry about any of this. But if you are using a self-hosted cart, make sure to disable the "store card information" feature in your configuration panel.

## Dealing With Fraudulent Orders

The possibility of fraudulent orders can be scary when you are starting out, but with some common sense and a bit of caution you can prevent the vast majority of losses due to fraud.

## The Address Verification System

The most common and widely used fraud prevention measure is the AVS, or address verification system. When the AVS feature is enabled, customers must enter the address on file with their credit card for the transaction to be approved. This helps prevent thieves with just the raw credit card number from successfully making purchases online. Fraud is rare for orders that pass the AVS check and are shipped to the customers' billing addresses.

The vast majority of fraudulent ecommerce orders occur when the billing and shipping addresses are different. In these cases, a thief enters the card owner's address as the billing address and enters a separate shipping address for the goods. Unfortunately, if you don't allow customers to ship to addresses other than the billing address, you will lose out on a lot of legitimate orders. But by allowing it, you are at risk for fraudulent orders that YOU will have to pay for. If you ship an order to an address other than the cardholder's address, the credit card company will make you foot the bill in the event of fraud.

Fortunately, fraudsters tend to follow patterns that make it easier to spot illegitimate orders before they ship. Individually, these signs won't help you flag a fraudulent order, but if you see two or three of them you should investigate:

- **Different Billing and Shipping**—Again, more than 95% of all fraudulent orders will have different billing and shipping addresses.

- **Different Names**—Different names on the billing and shipping addresses could be a red flag for fraudulent orders. That, or a gift purchase.

- **Unusual Email Addresses**—Most people have email addresses incorporating some part of their name, allowing you to match part of an email address to a customer's name. But if you see an address like dfssdfsdf@gmail.com, there's a good chance it's a made-up address and is one sign of fraud.

- **Expedited Shipping**—Since they're charging everything to someone else's card, fraudsters will often pick the fastest—and most expensive—delivery method. It also reduces the amount of time you have to catch them before the item is delivered.

If you spot an order you suspect is fraudulent, simply pick up the phone. Fraudsters almost never put their real number on an order. If the order is legitimate, you will likely have a 30-second discussion with someone that clears everything up. If not, you will get a dead number or someone who has no idea that she ordered a 25-foot boat scheduled for overnight delivery. At that point, you can cancel the order and issue a refund to avoid any chargebacks or problems.

# Understanding Chargebacks

When a customer calls his or her bank or credit card company to contest a charge made by you, you will receive what's called a "chargeback." Your payment processor will temporarily deduct the amount of the disputed charge from your account and ask you to prove that you delivered the goods or services to the customer. If you can't provide proof, you will lose the amount in question and be slapped with a $25 chargeback processing fee. If you rack up too many chargebacks relative to the volume of orders you are processing, you could even lose your merchant account.

The largest cause of chargebacks is usually fraud, but customers will also dispute a charge because they didn't recognize your business, forgot about the transaction or simply didn't like the product they received. We have seen it all.

When you receive a chargeback, you often have just a few days to respond, so you need to act quickly. To have a shot at getting your money back, you will need to provide documentation of the original order, tracking information showing delivery and likely a wholesale packing slip showing which items you purchased and shipped. If the contested charge was for a legitimate transaction, you will have a good chance of recovering the funds as long as you didn't make any untrue statements or promises in the course of the transaction.

Unfortunately, if the chargeback is related to an order with different billing and shipping addresses, you are almost certainly not going to win. Most processors will only compensate you for fraudulent orders shipped to the billing address on the card. In our businesses, we don't even bother responding to these kind of chargebacks because we know it's a waste of time.

# Dealing With Returns

Before writing your own return policy, you will want to make sure you know and understand how all your suppliers deal with returns. If they have a lax 45-day return window, you can afford to be generous with your terms. A strict return policy from just one supplier can cause you to re-evaluate the terms you can afford to have in place.

When a customer needs to return an item, the process will look like this:

1.  A customer contacts you to request a return.

2.  You request an RMA (return merchandise authorization) number from your supplier.

3.  The customer mails back the merchandise to your supplier, noting the RMA # on the address.

4.  The supplier refunds your account for the wholesale price of the merchandise.

5.  You refund the customer for the full price of the merchandise.

It's not always this straightforward, however. The following can complicate returns:

## Restocking Fees

Some suppliers will charge a restocking fee, which is essentially a surcharge for having to return an item. Even if your supplier charges these fees, we strongly recommend not having them be a part of your return policy. They seem outdated and unfriendly toward customers. Although you may have to eat a fee here and there, you will likely recoup that expense in more customers who decide to do business with you.

## Defective Items

The only thing worse than receiving a defective item is having to pay additional postage to return it. Most dropshipping suppliers won't cover return postage for defective items. In their minds, they didn't manufacture the item so they aren't liable for defects. They simply view it as a risk of selling products to a retail market.

You, however, should always compensate your customers for the return shipping fees for defective items if you are interested in building a reputable business. Again, this is a fee you won't be able to pass along to anyone, but it's part of the cost of running a quality dropshipping business. Unless you have your own UPS or FedEx account, it can be difficult to print a pre-paid shipping label for customers so you may need to issue a return shipping refund to compensate them for their out-of-pocket expense. However you do it, make sure you compensate them somehow.

If the defective item is relatively inexpensive, it often makes sense to just ship the customer a new product without requiring them to return the old one. This has a number of advantages compared to making them return the old item, including:

1.  **It Can Be Cost Effective**—It doesn't make sense to pay $10 to return an item that only costs you $12 from your wholesaler. You will get a $2 net credit, but it's not worth it for the hassle to your customer, supplier and staff.

2.  **The Customer Is Blown Away**—How often do companies simply ship out a new product without needing an old one back? Almost never. You will score major points and may land a customer for life. Also, the customer will get the new product much faster than if the old one had to be returned to the warehouse before the new item could be shipped.

3.  **Your Supplier May Pay for Shipping**—Suppliers won't pay for return shipping on a defective product, but most will pay to have a new replacement sent to the customer. Because they'll be paying for return shipping anyway, most suppliers can be talked into covering the shipping on a replacement product that you simply purchase separately. Plus, many are glad to duck the hassle of processing the return.

If a customer wants to return a non-defective product for a refund, most companies will expect the buyer to pay for the return freight. This is a fairly reasonable policy. If you are willing to offer free returns on everything, you will definitely stand out (and companies like Zappos have made this part of their unique business model). But it can get expensive, and most customers will understand that you shouldn't have to cough up return shipping fees simply because they ordered a product they ultimately didn't want.

## Shipping Issues

Calculating shipping rates can be a big mess for dropshipping merchants. With so many different products shipping from multiple locations, it's difficult to accurately calculate shipping rates for orders.

There are three types of shipping rates you can use:

**Real-Time Rates**—With this method, your shopping cart will use the collective weight of all items purchased and the shipping destination to get an actual real-time quote. This is very accurate but can be difficult to compute for shipments from multiple warehouses.

**Per-Type Rates**—Using a per-type method, you will set flat shipping rates based on the types of products ordered. So all small widgets would ship for a flat $5 rate, while all large widgets would be $10 to ship.

**Flat-Rate Shipping**—As the name implies, you'd charge one flat rate for all shipments, regardless of type. You could even offer free shipping on all orders. This method is the easiest to implement but is the least accurate in reflecting actual shipping costs.

When it comes to shipping, it's important to refer to the overarching principles about dropshipping that we listed at the outset of this chapter. Specifically, we want to find a solution that emphasizes simplicity over perfection, especially if we're just starting out.

Some merchants will spend days—or weeks—struggling to properly configure automated shipping rules for a store that has yet to generate a sale. Instead, they should focus on other issues like marketing and customer service, and quickly implement a shipping policy that makes sense from an overall level. Then, once they start to grow, they can invest in a more exact system. With this philosophy, it's often best to estimate an average shipping fee and set that as your overall flat rate. You will probably lose money on some orders but make it back on others.

Even if you could implement a system that passed along extra shipping fees based on supplier location, would you really want to? Most customers balk at excessive shipping fees, especially when they assume their order is originating from one location. Instead, try to limit multiple shipments by using suppliers with overlapping inventory and by being selective about the items you sell. This is a much more practical and simple long-term solution.

## International Shipments

International shipping has become easier but it's still not as straightforward as domestic shipping. When you ship internationally, you will need to consider and/or deal with:

- Different weight and length limitations for different countries.

- Additional charges from suppliers for processing international orders.

- The added expense of resolving problematic orders due to higher shipping fees.

- Excessive costs for shipping large and/or heavy items.

Is the hassle worth it? It depends on the market you are in and the margins you earn. If you sell small items with higher margins, the increased market reach may make it worthwhile to deal with the hassle and expense of offering international shipments. For others—especially merchants selling larger or heavier items—the added benefit won't be worth the expense and inconvenience.

## Picking a Carrier

Selecting the right carrier is important, as it can save you a significant amount of money. In the U.S., the largest decision you will need to make is between UPS/FedEx and the U.S. Postal Service.

**UPS/FedEx**—These privately run giants are great for shipping large, heavy packages domestically. Their rates for big shipments will be significantly lower than those charged by the USPS.

**U.S. Postal Service**—If you are shipping small, lightweight items you can't beat the rates offered by the USPS. After dropshipping fees, the cheapest UPS shipping fee you are likely to see is around $10, while you can often ship items for $5 or less through the post office. The post office tends to be a better choice for sending international shipments, especially smaller ones.

When setting up your shipping options, consider categorizing them by shipping time ("Within 5 Days" or "Within 3 Days"), as this gives you the flexibility to pick the carrier that's the most economical for each order and delivery time.

## Providing Customer Support

Take it from us: Managing all your customer emails, requests and returns in an Excel spreadsheet is not ideal. As excellent as Excel is, it's not built to handle customer support. Similarly, as your business and team grow, managing support with a single email inbox also quickly breaks down and leads to problems and service lapses.

Implementing a help desk is one of the best things you can do to ensure quality service for your customers. Help desk software comes in a number of different forms, but all provide a centralized location to manage your customer support correspondence and issues. Most desks make it easy to assign issues to team members and maintain communication history among all related parties.

A few popular options to choose from include:

**Help Scout**—Less cluttered than other desks, Help Scout treats each issue as an email and removes all the traditionally appended ticket information that customers see with support requests. Instead, support tickets appear like standard emails to customers, creating a more personalized experience.

**Zendesk**—Highly customizable and powerful, Zendesk offers a variety of tools and integrations and is one of the most popular help desks available. It takes some customization but is very powerful once it's tailored to your company.

**Desk**—Backed by well-known SalesForce, Desk's 'Universal Inbox' allows you to interact with your customers across numerous channels from one streamlined interface.

**Kayako**—Kayako boasts an all-in-one platform that offers built-in live chat, phone call and remote support issue management alongside traditional ticket-based support.

## Offering Phone Support

Deciding whether to offer phone support can be a tricky decision. It's obviously a great way to provide real-time support but is one of the most expensive support methods. If you are bootstrapping a business while working your 9 to 5, you won't be able to handle calls. But if you are working full-time on your business—or have a staff member who can—it might be a feasible option. If you are unable to staff a phone throughout the day, you can always have your phone number ring through to voicemail and return customer calls later. This isn't a perfect solution but can be a good compromise.

You should consider the type of products you will be selling when thinking about how to offer phone support. If you are a diamond boutique selling jewelry in the $1,000 to $5,000 range, many customers won't be comfortable placing an order that large without talking to a real person. However, if you are selling products in the $25 to $50 range, most people will feel comfortable buying without phone support, assuming you've built a professional, information-rich website.

If you do decide to offer phone support, think through strategic ways to do so. Slapping a large 800 number on the top of every page can lead to a surfeit of low-value phone calls that cost more to support than they're worth. Instead, consider adding your number in more strategic places like the Contact Us and Shopping Cart pages, where you know the visitor has a high probability of purchasing.

Regardless of how you decide to handle sales requests, you should always be willing to call customers after the sale to resolve any issues that arise. There is nothing wrong with carefully evaluating the best ways to offer pre-sale support, but when it comes to taking care of people who have purchased from you, you should never refuse to help them on the phone.

The following services can help you set up a toll-free number and sales line:

**Grasshopper**—Grasshopper offers phone services and is geared toward smaller businesses and entrepreneurs. You can get a toll-free number, unlimited extensions, call forwarding and voicemail for a reasonable monthly fee (around $25).

**RingCentral**—RingCentral is the 800-pound gorilla in the VoIP and 800-number space. It's flexible interface lets you set up custom routing rules and extensions and the service can scale quite nicely with your business as it grows.

# CHAPTER 8

# The Key Elements of Success

WE HAVE COVERED A bunch of information so far, discussing everything from the fundamentals of dropshipping to the intricacies of picking a niche and running your business. By now, you should have enough of a foundation to confidently get started researching and launching your own dropshipping business.

With so much to consider, it's easy to get overwhelmed and lose track of what's really important. That's why we created this list of the crucial elements to success. These are the core "must-do" actions that will make or break your new venture. If you can successfully execute these, you will be able to get a lot of other things wrong and still have a great chance at success.

## 1. Add Value

Having a solid plan for how you can add value to your customers is the most crucial success factor. This is important for all businesses, but much more so in the world of dropshipping, where you will be competing with legions of other "me too" shops carrying similar products.

With dropshipping, it's easy to think you are selling customers a product. But successful small merchants understand that it's not only the product they offer—they're selling insights, information and solutions. You think you are an ecommerce merchant but you are actually in the information business.

So how are you going to add value and help solve problems for your customers? You should have a clear answer to this question before launching your business. If you are unsure, spend some time re-reading **Chapter 4**, which discusses the topic in depth. If you are struggling to answer this question for a given niche, you may want to consider picking a different market.

If you are not able to add value through quality information and guidance, the only thing you are left to compete on is price. While this has been a successful strategy for Walmart, it's not going to help you build a successful dropshipping business.

## 2. Focus on Marketing and SEO

Coming in a close second to adding value as a key success factor is being able to drive traffic to your new site. The number one problem and frustration new ecommerce merchants face is a lack of traffic to their websites. Too many merchants slave away for months on the perfect site only to launch it to a world that has no idea it exists.

Marketing and driving traffic is absolutely essential to the success of your business and is difficult to outsource well, especially if you have a small budget and are bootstrapping your business. You need to take the personal initiative to develop your own SEO, marketing, outreach and guest posting skills.

This is particularly crucial during the first 6 to 12 months, when no one knows who you are. Following your site launch, you need to dedicate at least 75% of your time on marketing, SEO and traffic generation for at least 4 to 6 months—that's right, 4 to 6 months. Once you've established a solid marketing foundation, you can scale back and coast a bit on the work you put in. But early on, it's impossible to place too much emphasis on marketing.

If you are not a marketing or SEO expert yet, the following resources and blogs are a great way to get started:

## SEO Resources:

- **SEOmoz**: One of the most popular SEO communities online. Their beginners guide to SEO is a particularly great resource for those starting out.

- **SearchEngineLand**: Extremely prolific SEO blog, with dozens of new posts each day.

- **SEOBook**: A popular SEO blog and the home of a paid private community for SEO professionals.

- **Distilled:** This marketing and SEO agency has a top-notch blog and a number of quality training courses and guides, many of which are free.

- **SEERInteractive.com**: Lots of quality SEO tips in this blog from a well-known agency.

## Marketing Resources:

- **Hubspot Blog**: Advice on everything inbound marketing related, from driving traffic with email to social media tips.

- **Seth Godin's Blog:** Solid high-level advice on marketing and building an audience.

- **QuickSprout**: A blog by well-known entrepreneur Neil Patel dedicated largely to marketing, SEO and traffic generation.

- **KISSmetrics Blog**: In-depth marketing posts with a slant toward analytics, usability and conversion.

- **SparringMind**: How to use behavioral psychology to help influence customers and market your business.

- **CopyBlogger**: Content marketing tips with an emphasis on writing effective, compelling copywriting.

- **Mixergy**: Interviews with successful entrepreneurs in the technology and online fields. Not focused exclusively on marketing, but lots of applicable information for aspiring entrepreneurs including marketing and early-stage advice.

## Ecommerce Marketing Resources:

- **Shopify Blog:** A comprehensive ecommerce blog with frequent posts on how to effectively promote and market your online store.

- **eCommerceFuel:** Tips from an active ecommerce entrepreneur on how to found, grow and market online stores. Written specifically for individual store owners and smaller stores.

- **GetElastic:** SEO and marketing information from an ecommerce perspective.

# 3. Specialize!

Almost every successful dropshipping store we encounter has one thing in common: It specializes in a certain product or niche. The more that stores specialize, the more successful they tend to be.

You don't want to just sell backpacks. You want to sell backpacks designed for around-the-world travelers obsessed with lightweight gear. You don't want to just sell security camera equipment. You want to focus on security systems for gas stations.

Many think narrowing their focus limits their potential customer base and will cost them sales. Just the opposite is true. Specializing allows you to communicate more effectively with your customers, stand out more easily from the competition and compete against a smaller field. Specializing is rarely a bad move to make in a dropshipping venture.

If you are launching a store in a new niche you probably won't know what segment of your customers to focus on—and that's OK. But as you gain experience with your customers you should identify the segment that's the most profitable and that allows you to add the most value. Then, try to position your business to focus exclusively on those customers' needs and problems. You will be amazed at how your conversion rates skyrocket even if you are charging a premium price.

Remember: If everyone is your customer, then no one is. Specialization makes it easier to differentiate yourself, charge a premium price and concentrate your marketing efforts more effectively.

## 4. Have a Long-Term Perspective

Building a dropshipping business is like building anything else of value: It takes a significant level of commitment and investment over time. Yet for some reason people assume they can build a passive six-figure income with dropshipping after a few months of part-time work. That's just not the way it works.

It will realistically take take at least a year to build a business that generates an average full-time income.

It is also important to understand that the first few months are the most difficult. You will struggle with doubts, run into issues with your website and will likely have an underwhelming website launch that generates zero sales. Understand that this is normal. Rome wasn't built in a day, and neither were any successful dropshipping businesses.

If you mentally prepare for a challenging beginning and don't expect to get rich overnight, you will be much more likely to stick with your business until it becomes a success.

## 5. Offer Outstanding Service

The Internet has always been a fairly transparent place, but the recent rise of social media has made your business reputation even more important to your success online. If you don't treat your customers well, they'll often let the entire world know—including many potential customers.

The biggest customer service risk for dropshipping merchants is having tunnel vision on per-order profits and losses when fulfillment issues go awry. It is critical to accept that dropshipping can get messy, that you will be paying to clean up some messes, and that you shouldn't always try to pass these on to your customer. If you aren't occasionally losing money on individual orders to make customers happy, you are probably not providing very good service.

Having happy customers is some of the best marketing you can do. As is true in all businesses, it's much easier to make a sale to a satisfied customer than to try to convince a new prospect to buy. If you treat your customers exceptionally well, they're likely to spread the word and refer others your way. With top-notch service, you can build a business where repeat customers generate much of your revenue.

Making customer service a priority set your dropshipping business up for success, so ensure it's a priority from the outset.

# 6. Don't Get Hung Up on the Details

As much as we'd love to tell you that Shopify is the only service you will be able to succeed with, it's simply not true. Sure, it's a world-class ecommerce platform, but realistically you can be successful with almost any shopping cart. Similarly, your company name, logo, theme or email marketing service aren't going to determine your success.

What makes a business successful are the things we just talked about: adding value, marketing, outstanding customer service, specializing and a long-term commitment. Still, new merchants will spend weeks— Sometimes months—struggling to decide which shopping cart to go with, or what color their logo should be. That's valuable time better spent developing the core aspects of the business.

Do your research and make an informed decision, but don't let small decisions paralyze you.

## 7. The Most Important Step

The most important step—the one that most people never take—is to actually get started building your business. This is the hardest thing for most people and it's usually a result of fear and uncertainty.

It's a common misconception that successful entrepreneurs have a rock-solid certainty about their business at the outset. When you dig a little deeper, you will find that most had fears and reservations about how things would turn out. Yet they moved forward with their plan despite these doubts.

If you are serious about building your own dropshipping business, you will need to do the same. Do your research, evaluate your options and then move forward with that information in spite of your fears and reservations. It's what entrepreneurs do.

## 8. Making Your First Sale

Finally, once your dropshipping business is up and running your number one priority will be making your first sale. Have you ever walked into a bar, restaurant, or other small business and saw money framed and mounted on the wall like a trophy or work of fine art? For many businesses that first sale, first dollar earned is a monument, marking the transition to a real revenue-generating concern. Unfortunately, brand new online retailers sometimes open to something like the sound of crickets chirping. Here are 16 ways to make your first online sale even before Google has bothered to notice you:

## Tell Family & Friends

Imitate the Avon ladies, Tupperware queens, and Pampered Chefs of multi-level marketing and tell all of your family and friends about your new ecommerce store. Encourage them to share a link or two on Facebook, Twitter, Google+, and Pinterest. Remember, you're not just asking them to make a purchase, you're asking them to share your online store with their network—which can be extremely valuable.

## Use Google Adwords

Pay-per-click (PPC) marketing, at its core, is the act of buying site traffic. Although PPC marketing can be nuanced, it is a pretty sure fired way to get site visitors and, thereby, sales. Finding the right audience across millions of websites can be difficult and when you're paying per click, the costs can add up. Be sure to learn some Google AdWords best practices before ramping up your spend too much.

## Give Stuff Away

Giving products away may not seem like a smart way to sell something, but there are two clever ways to turn giveaways into real sales.

You can gain hundreds, even thousands of email subscribers by hosting a product giveaway before or after your online store opens. Ask visitors to register to enter the contest and give bonus entries for sharing the contest on social media networks or forwarding it to friends. Once the site launches, or when the contest ends, send a promotional email offering a discount.

Search Google for the influencers in your industry. Say you're selling a cool new gadget, find the reporters, blogs, and magazines that may be interested in your product and send them a free sample with a short description of what your product and online store is all about. Big businesses have been doing this for ages, and it works if done correctly. Just don't expect a huge response from this tactic, even if you only get 1 article as a result, the campaign should be considered a success.

## Make an Infographic

Informational graphics, better known as infographics, visually display data in a way that makes it easy to understand. This form of data communication has become very popular recently. Have a designer create an infographic relevant to the products your store carries.

For example, if you sell hiking boots you could publish an infographic about the miles of open, public trails that might show how the number of miles of trails has changed over time or in comparison to other regions. The inforgraphic could then be released on a paid news service like *iReach* or a free design "show-and-tell" platform like dribbble. Dozens of publications could republish the graphic, each one linking back to the store.

## Submit to Product Feeds

Sites like The Find, Nextag, Shopzilla, and Google Merchant, aggregate product information and prices so that consumers can find and, let's be frank, compare prices more readily. Adding a feed to one of these sites and sometimes paying a small fee could send a parade of new customers to your online store, helping to secure an initial sale.

## Embrace Video

When the marketers at Seattle-based Replyboard launched their service, which screens Craigslist replies, they released four videos showing

Replyboard pranksters responding to Craigslist ads. One video features a man randomly taking a shower at a seller's home. It's pretty hilarious.

While it might not be a great idea to "punk" potential customers, video can be a very powerful way to promote a new business, and in the case of an ecommerce business, garner sales. You can also consider adding ecommerce product videos to your online store to better display some of your more popular products.

## Ask Vendors for Some Love

Distributors and manufacturers will often help new retailers by including the startup in dealer listings or mentioning the new retailer on social media sites. Don't be afraid to ask them for some assistance while you're building your business.

## Get Interviewed

Merchants are frequently experts in a particular industry. If you sell handmade shirts and you're knowledgeable in men's fashion, why not approach media outlets about providing them with expert comment on fashion. Reporters are often on the hunt for industry experts, and you will often get the opportunity to mention the company you own or represent.

## Make an Awesome Blog

Content marketing is the technique of attracting site visitors (read potential customers) by providing good quality content, like how-to blog posts. There are a few key ingredients to improve your ecommerce store's blog and make it something worth sharing: Offer good and relevant content, make sure it's visually appealing, show your products in action, keep it short and snappy, and show them behind the scenes.

## Use Amazon Product Ads

Amazon lets online retailers place ads right in the context of an Amazon product detail page. Since the people who see your ad are already on Amazon.com looking to make a purchase, the conversion rate on these ads can be much higher than traditional PPC.

## Hand Out Business Cards

Every online store owner should have business cards. Get some cards made, make sure they are stylish and reflect your store design. Remember, your store URL should be front and center. Once you have your cards, hand them out to everyone!

## Rev Up Social Media

You have probably read a million blog articles and books about social media marketing for a reason—it works. Make sure you have a strong presence on all the usual suspects: Twitter, Facebook, and Pinterest. Start conversations about your industry, and also inject yourself into conversations already happening, and you'll quickly grow to become an influencer and a thought leader. It's amazing how much traffic you can drive through social media. If you keep growing your social presence it won't be long until your following start to convert to customers.

## Create a Coupon Code

Everyone loves a deal. You may be surprised how many people shop by typing "_____ coupon code" into Google. Create a coupon code for your online store then head over to a site like RetailMeNot or RedFlagDeals and post your deal.

## Consider an Affiliate Program

With an affiliate program you can pay people to share and promote your products. Essentially, you sign up with a service like Commission Junction or ShareASale and then you'll pay the "affiliate" a certain commission on each sale they bring you. These sites can be expensive and time consuming so they're not for everyone, but for certain products it's worth a shot.

## Facebook Advertising

Facebook advertising can be a great way to access a very targeted audience. Lets say you sell jewelry, with Facebook Advertising you can target people who have "jewelry" or "watches" or "bracelets" with custom banners that have a message specifically to their interests. Similar to Google AdWords, advertising on Facebook is PPC.

## Be Patient

If you were launching a brick and mortar store or restaurant you probably wouldn't expect your business to be profitable for the first little while. Same goes with ecommerce—it takes time, so be patient.

# Appendix:
# My Corporate Escape Story

*This is the first person account of how co-author Andrew Youderian made his escape from corporate America to launch his first ecommerce business with dropshipping, and the effect it had on his life.*

It was 5:00 on a Sunday, and I still had hours of work to do at the office. My girlfriend—who lived nine hours away and was in town for a rare visit—was sitting alone in my apartment, anxiously waiting for me to finish (and likely reconsidering her choice to date me).

How did I end up in this position? I never really intended to go into investment banking, a field notorious for long hours and insane work schedules. But it was an enticing job right out of college, offering solid job experience and the chance to really see how large businesses worked.

Our schedule wasn't nearly as strenuous as many of the bigger investment banks, where 100-hour work weeks are the norm. Still, the

60- to 80-hour weeks, unpredictable schedule and inability to commit to people and/or plans quickly grew draining, especially for work that I didn't love.

I made the decision to quit and started to save as much money as possible. I kept my beater college car longer than necessary in order to save more money—a car so hideous I opted to park it blocks from the office. I banked 100% of the bonuses I received and earned a reputation around the office as a bit of a miser. In the small amount of spare time I did have, I read Tim Ferriss' "The Four-Hour Work Week" and started dreaming about my future plans. I was laying the foundation for my escape.

In November of 2007, I quit. It's both an exhilarating and slightly terrifying feeling to leave a good job to start your own business. After a solo cross-county road trip, I settled down to start building my future. I didn't know exactly what I wanted to do. I did, however, know the required characteristics I wanted my new venture to have. It needed to:

- Offer a high risk-to-reward ratio
- Require little capital
- Be scalable
- Be location-independent

It's amazing how a total lack of income motivates you to action. After exploring a number of potential ideas, I quickly settled on e-commerce and dropshipping as a business model that fit all my criteria. I opened up a bank account with $1,500, created an LLC and picked a niche: short-range radio equipment.

It's about this time I think my mother lost total faith in me. Already somewhat distraught that I'd quit my job, she now had to let friends and family know her son had left the finance world to hawk radios via the internet. To be honest, I had a few doubts myself, but because my research methodology indicated radios might be a viable niche, I took a leap of faith and launched my first ecommerce business, Right Channel Radios.

Within a month I had my website online and live. Bootstrapped and designed by myself, it wasn't going to win any awards, but it was a working prototype that could take orders and test my idea's viability. Shortly after launch, I received my first order. As any business owner will tell you, few things compare to the thrill of your first sale, and it provided an incredible motivational boost.

Over the following months, I threw myself entirely into growing and improving my business. I hungrily learned as much as I could about online marketing, SEO (search engine optimization), my customers and my new market. Sales began to grow, albeit sporadically. My girlfriend (now wife) Annie could tell from my mood each evening how orders had been that day. I continued to bootstrap the business, reinvesting the earnings and my own sweat, but never adding any additional equity apart from my original $1,500 deposit.

Slowly but surely everything began to pay off. Within a year, I was making enough to support myself and Annie. I hired a part-time virtual assistant (VA) to help manage business operations. Within two years, I launched a second e-commerce site, TrollingMotors.net, and shortly thereafter hired my first full-time local employee.

With a great team in place to run most of the daily operations, I decided to take a break from growing the business to pursue a goal of mine: long-term international travel. So in February of 2011, Annie and I departed for a seven-month working vacation that took us to more than 20 countries.

The trip was financed largely by over 2 million frequent flier miles I had generated by paying to fulfill orders from my stores.

After an incredible trip, we returned home in November. Despite being gone seven out of 12 months, it was a record year for revenues with my businesses collectively generating $1 million in sales and setting the stage for well above that in 2012. It was my best year ever in terms of income, and I earned significantly more than I ever did investment banking.

Five years and numerous businesses later, I have learned a tremendous amount that I have incorporated into this book. My hope in writing is to help others who, like me in my banking days, want to build a better life for themselves through entrepreneurship. While my path has been unorthodox, it's one that can be re-created by anyone with the determination to make it happen. This isn't to say that building your own e-commerce business is easy—far from it. I think with entrepreneurial "success" stories, it's tempting to indulge the good and downplay the bad and I want to intentionally avoid that.

One of the most undiscussed factors to entrepreneurial success is the importance of creating a foundation to succeed from. When I quit my job, I had a large cash cushion that gave me the flexibility to take a chance and start my business. But saving this cushion took years or sacrifice—not something that was necessarily easy or fun.

Starting my first site was hard, really hard. It required a lot of work, much of it tedious, with little visible success for the first few months. Staying motivated with little to show for your efforts is extremely challenging in the early days of a venture.

Ultimately, business success of any kind, ecommerce included, requires significant sacrifice and work, but I'm here to tell you that the investment is absolutely worth it. I believe there has never been a better time in history for individuals to start their own businesses. For online ventures, the risks are small and the rewards significant. If you decide to head down the same path I have, I hope the information we have shared in this book will help you along the way.

# Glossary

**Address Verification System (AVS):** Built to fight payment card fraud, the payment card Address Verification System compares the billing address a user submits during a card-not-present transaction with the billing address on record. AVS is one of several payment card fraud prevention systems.

**Affiliate:** A publisher or site owner that forwards qualified web traffic to an online merchant on a pay-for-performance basis is called an affiliate in the context of online marketing.

**Affiliate Links:** A universal (uniform) resource locator (URL) that includes an affiliate's identification number and additional information that makes it easier for merchants to track affiliate activity is an affiliate link.

**Amazon:** In the retail context, Amazon is a multi-national online retailer with a market capitalization in excess of $128 billion U.S. as of January

2013. Amazon also hosts a marketplace wherein other Internet purveyors may display and sell products, and offers several software-as-a-service and infrastructure-as-a-service solutions for business.

**Application Programming Interface (API):** An API is a protocol created to allow separate software solutions to communicate over a relatively simple interface. Developers will often use APIs to connect or integrate systems and services.

**Authorization:** A payment card transaction performed specifically to determine if the payment account has sufficient funds to complete a given transaction.

**Authorized Distributor:** A manufacturer-approved or -designated distributor able to sell products in quantity to commercial customers like Internet retailers.

**Authorized Retailer:** A manufacturer-approved or -designated retailer able to sell products directly to consumers.

**Better Business Bureau:** A non-profit organization in Canada and the United States that is focused on trust in advertising. The organization responds to consumer inquiries about business reliability, and accredits businesses. Accredited online merchants may display a Better Business Bureau badge.

**Bing:** Microsoft's search engine, Bing, displays results in response to a user's search query. The site uses a complex and secret algorithm to select which sites to display in response to a particular search. Bing also offers a pay-per-click advertising platform, and allows merchants to offer a discount to shoppers.

**Blog:** A blog is an online journal or publication that includes relatively short, discrete articles, called posts, that are typically organized by date with the most recent posts first. Frequently, blogs allow readers to add comments to posts. The term blog is a combination of "web" and "log." At first, blogs tended to be personal journals or opinion sites, but the term has come to include an array of different types of publications. In the ecommerce context, blogs are frequently used as a marketing tool, and may be included in a merchant's social media or content marketing campaigns.

**Bootstrapping:** In business, bootstrapping is the concept of self-funding a new company, meaning that a business pays its operating expenses either with profits or from its founder's own investments, rather than accepting external capital.

**Bounce Rate:** An Internet marketing term used to describe the percentage of site visitors that arrive at a single page on a given website, and then leave (bounce) from that same page without visiting any other page on the site.

**Brick & Click Store:** A retail outlet or business with at least one physical location and at least one ecommerce enabled website.

**Brick & Mortar Store:** A retail outlet or business with at least one physical location.

**Business Structure:** A company's legal status or organization. Often refers to incorporation.

**Call-to-Action:** A phrase, button, link or other site element that specifically asks a visitor to take some action, including purchasing a product, registering, subscribing or similar.

**Canonicalization:** The practice of selecting preferred URLs for a specific set of content. Many modern sites allow content to be accessed from a number of URLs, including URLs that may contain session or query information. Canonicalization helps to manage which of those URLs search engines index and credit.

**Canonical URL:** The canonical meta tag that directs search engines to index the preferred URL for site content that is available from multiple URLs.

**Capture:** The process of securing payments from a payment process after an authorization.

**Chargeback:** When an issuing back forcibly reverses a transaction, taking funds from a merchant and returning those funds to a consumer. Nearly all chargebacks are the result of a consumer complaint, including claims that the transaction was not authorized, not fulfilled, or not as described. Chargebacks may also affect the rate that merchants pay to process card-not-present transactions.

**Comma Separated Values (CSV):** A file type that stores data values. CSV files are often used to transfer product feeds.

**Confirmed Shipping Address:** The phrase confirmed shipping address may have two similar but distinct meanings in the ecommerce context. Confirmed Shipping Address may simply be an address that actually exists based on a review from a package carrier like FedEx or the United States Postal Service. The phrase may also refer to a shipping address that a particular consumer has either registered with a payment processor or used successfully in a prior transaction with a particular merchant.

**Content Management System (CMS):** A software solution that makes it possible to create, edit, maintain, publish, and display content on the

Internet from a single interface or administration tool. In the online retailing context, a CMS may be used to manage a stores product catalog.

**Conversion:** A marketing term that describes when a user or visitor completes some action or achieves some marketing goal. More specifically, conversion is often used to describe when a site visitor converts to a customer, making a purchase.

**Cookie:** A very small file saved on a user's computer or mobile device for the purpose of storing information related to the user's interaction with a particular site.

**Corporation:** A distinct legal entity and business structure, wherein the business is separate from its shareholders.

**Customer Relationship Management (CRM):** A software solution specifically devoted to organizing, synchronizing, and automating a business' customer relationships.

**CSS:** A stylesheet language used to describe the "look and feel" of a site written in HTML. CSS allows a page's presentation to be separated from its structure, making updates and maintenance easier. CSS stands for *Cascading Style Sheet*.

**Delivery Confirmation (DC):** A service offered by many package carriers, like the United States Postal Service and FedEx, that provides the shipper with information about when a package was delivered. This is not the same as when a customer signs for a package.

**Directories:** Sites that list and link to other sites, including online stores, are referred to as directories.

**Discount Code:** A series of numbers and/or letters that an online shopper may enter at checkout to get a discount or other special offer. Discount codes may also be called coupon codes.

**Distributor:** A distribution business that inventories products from a number of manufacturers and sells to many retailers. Often distributors are able to offer shorter lead times than manufacturers and may sell in smaller quantities. It is common for distributors to charge a premium over a manufacturer-direct price for the service and convenience provided.

**Domain:** The root address for a web page.

**Dropshipping:** A fulfillment strategy wherein the retailer does not actually inventory the dropshipped product, but instead passes the shipping address to either the manufacturer, or a distributor that actually ships the purchased items directly to the customer.

**Dutch Auction:** Depending on context, the term Dutch Auction may have more than one specific meaning. At its simplest, a Dutch Auction is an auction that starts with a high price that is lowered incrementally until a bid is placed or a reserve (minimum) price is met. Also, the term may describe an auction wherein more than one of an item is for sale, each item may sell for a separate price, so that one buyer may take two of an item for $1, while the next buyer takes three items at 90 cents each. Finally, a Dutch Auction can refer to an auction wherein many items or lots are for sale, but all will sell for the same value. All bids are considered and a common low bid price is determined for the sale of all items.

**eBay:** A online auction and shopping website, best known for its consumer-to-consumer sales. Many online merchants also use eBay as a sales channel.

**Ecommerce:** Buying and selling products over electronic networks, including the Internet or mobile applications. The term may apply specifically to electronic transactions or more generally to the online retailing and online business.

**EIN:** The United States Internal Revenue Service may issue a business an Employer Identification Number (EIN), which is also known as a Federal Tax Identification Number. The EIN is used for tax collection and certain types of tax or sales reporting.

**Expedited Shipping:** A shipping option that features reduced handling or transit times. Customers frequently pay a premium in order to ensure that an ordered item arrives more quickly.

**Exporting:** The practice of selling items to wholesale or retail customers in another country.

**Fraud:** Intentional deception for the purpose of gain.

**Fulfillment:** In ecommerce, fulfillment is the process of completing an order. The term may also be applied to third-party companies that inventory products and ship orders on behalf of an online store.

**Google:** The leading search engine provider, Google displays search results using a complex and secret algorithm that considers many factors. The company seeks to show its users the best possible results. Google also provides other services, including a pay-per-click advertising network, payment processing solutions, product discovery tools, and an excellent analytics platform.

**Google Keyword Tool:** A free keyword suggestion tool included in the Google AdWords Platform. The tool uses data from the many searches conducted on the Google search engine to suggest keywords for a given URL and category.

**Google Trends:** A search engine tool that shows how often a particular term or keyword is searched for on Google. Results are shown in a relative scale, making the tool well suited for comparing keywords or phrases. Trends will also show where searches came from and how search volume for a particular keyword has changed over time.

**HTML (Hyper Text Markup Language):** A markup language specifically created for displaying web pages and applications in web browsers. Like other markup languages, HTML annotates a document, describing its layout and syntax.

**Inventory:** The value or quantity of a retailer's current stock of products.

**JavaScript:** A scripting language—ECMAscript—used to make web pages interactive and dynamic.

**Landing Pages:** In the online marketing context, a landing page is a single web page that is displayed in response to a particular call to action. Landing pages are often shown in response to a link in a pay-per-click ad, a link in an email, or a specific URL shown in offline advertising. Landing pages include content meant to meet the expectation set with the link a visitor clicked.

**Limited Liability Company (LLC):** A business structure that blends some of the best elements of a partnership and a corporation.

**Linking Root Domains:** In search engine optimization, when site A links to site B one or more times, site A is said to be a linking root domain.

Linking root domains — in the plural — are the total number of unique sites that link one or more times to a given website.

**Liquidation:** A sale intended to dispose of all of a given product line's inventory with the intention of not replenishing supplies.

**Liquidator:** A company that purchases closeout products for the purpose of resale.

**Listing Fees:** Marketplaces and online auction sites, like eBay, may charge a nominal listing fee for posting products.

**Logistics:** The management of products or other resources as they travel between a point of origin and a destination. In ecommerce, logistics might describe the process of transporting inventory to a merchant or the act of shipping orders to customers.

**Long Tail:** Posited in the October 2004 issue of Wired Magazine, the Long Tail is Chris Anderson's idea that markets and marketplaces, especially online, are moving away from mainstream, broad-appeal products toward niche products. In ecommerce, new retailers may find it easier and more cost effective to focus on niche products.

**Long-Tail Variations:** In search engine optimization and pay-per-click advertising, Long-Tail variations are keywords similar in meaning or root to other high-volume keywords, but less competitive. Long-Tail variations are often employed when a business is just starting out and cannot gain traction or afford to bid on top performing keywords.

**Long-Tail Traffic:** Website traffic derived from Long-Tail variation keywords or from niche searches and keywords in general.

**Manufacturer:** A company that makes goods for the purpose of sale.

**Manufacturer's Suggested Retail Price (MSRP):** The price at which a manufacturer recommends that retailers sell a given product.

**MAP Pricing:** Manufacturers may require retailers to sell or advertise a given product at a minimum price. This price floor is known as a minimum advertised price or a minimum acceptable price. Manufacturers vary in their MAP enforcement, with some cancelling retail dealer agreements, if sellers offer products below MAP.

**Margins:** The difference between what a retailer pays for a product and what the retailer's customer pays for the product. Margin calculations may consider only the cost of the goods sold or may take into account overhead and other variable costs.

**Meta Tags:** HTML tags that provide information about a web page, but do not necessarily impact how a page is displayed. Meta tag information is useful in search engine optimization and for use with some social media application programming interfaces.

**Minimum Order Size:** Manufacturers or distributors may require retailers to place orders that meet a minimum value or unit count. This requirement would be the minimum order size.

**Multi-Channel Retailing:** Retailing products through more than one channel where channels include online stores, online marketplaces like Amazon, physical stores, physical catalogs, and similar.

**Multivariate Testing:** In online marketing, a testing model that has marketers simultaneously test many variables in order to discover which variation in web page or ad content or design produces the best possible result. Simply put, prospects might see one of several variations of a page or online ad, while marketers measure which variation did the best job of achieving some stated goal, like making a sale.

**Net Profit:** The difference between a business' revenue and its costs—all of its costs. Net profit may be thought of as the money left over after every bill is paid.

**Net Terms:** Credit term that a supplier extends to a retailer, allowing the retailer to pay for purchased items some number of days after those items have been shipped. Often net terms are described as "net 30," "net 120," or similar where net 30 means that a retailer has 30 days to pay for an order after that order has shipped. Frequently, net terms will also include a discount so that 5/10 net 30 would mean that a retailer would receive a 5-percent discount if the bill was paid in 10 days or less, otherwise the bill is due in 30 days.

**Niche:** A distinct market segment.

**Open Site Explorer:** A SEOmoz link analysis tool created to help measure several aspects of a site search optimization and link quality.

**Order Fulfillment:** In ecommerce, order fulfillment is the process of completing an order, shipping a product or products to the customer. The term may also be applied to logistics companies that inventory products and ship orders on behalf of an online store.

**Organic:** In the context of search engine optimization and search engine marketing, organic results are those listings search engines show because of their relevance to a query, not because a site owner paid for an ad or paid to be featured.

**Outsource:** The process of contracting work to external, third-party organizations.

**Overhead:** The ongoing expenses associated with operating a business.

**PageRank:** Google's proprietary page ranking system that places emphasis on inbound links as a means of determining how important a given page is. PageRank can be measured on either a ten-point or 100-point scale.

**Patent:** Protection for some forms of intellectual property, granting the inventory exclusive right to manufacture, use, or sell an invention for a certain number of years.

**PayPal:** Founded in 1998, PayPal is a leading, worldwide payment processing company. The service can process payments for merchants.

**Pay Per Click (PPC):** An online advertising model wherein advertisers pay only when a prospect clicks on an advertisement and is directed to the advertiser's website. Google's AdWords platform is an example of pay-per-click promotion.

**Per-Order Fee:** When a manufacturer or distributor dropships an order directly to a customer on a retailers behave that manufacturer or distributor may change a per-order fee for processing.

**Preferred Supplier:** Some businesses will specify preferred suppliers, encouraging employees with purchase privileges to order specific categories of products from preferred suppliers. In the retail context, being a preferred supplier for a large organization may lead to additional sales.

**Profit Margin:** The difference between what a retailer pays for a product and what the retailer's customer pays for the product. Margin calculations may consider only the cost of the goods sold or may take into account overhead and other variable costs.

**Quantitative Metrics:** In online marketing, quantitative metrics are those measures that may be represented as numbers. Click-through rates, visitor counts, and time-on-site are all examples of quantitative metrics.

**Qualitative Metrics:** In online marketing, qualitative metrics seek to measure the quality of a customer interaction, and may be subjective in nature. A retailer, as an example, may implement a new product review campaign, compare reviews written before and after the campaign, awarding each review a qualitative score, and then use the relative scored to decide if the campaign was successful.

**Reseller:** A company that purchases goods or services for the purpose of resale not consumption. In web economics, a reseller may also be a form of affiliate marketer, promoting a rebranded service.

**Restocking Fees:** A fee charged to customers who are returning products. Often the restocking fee is subtracted from the customer's refund.

**Retailer:** A company that sells directly to the end consumer.

**Search Engine Marketing (SEM):** Online marketing aimed at increasing a given website's visibility on a search engine results page (SERP) by both optimizing the website for indexing and purchasing ads or paid inclusions.

**Search Engine Optimization (SEO):** The process of making a website easier for search engine bots to index and categorize.

**Search Engine Results Page (SERP):** A search engine web page displaying the list of responses to a particular search query.

**Shipping:** The process of physically moving merchandise form a point of origin, like a retailer's warehouse, to a destination, like a customer's home.

**Social Media:** Internet-based tools or websites that facilitate sharing of content, opinions, links, images, or videos between people.

**Social Media Marketing:** A branch of Internet marketing aimed at promoting products or service via social media. It may be thought of as web-based word-of-mouth marketing.

**Sole Proprietorship:** A business structure wherein a single individual both owns and runs the company. For the most part, there is not legal distinction between the owner and the business.

**Split Testing:** In online marketing, a testing model that has marketers simultaneously test two variables (often labeled A and B) in order to discover which variation in web page or ad content or design produces the best possible result.

**Supply Chain:** A network or system of businesses involved in moving a product from its manufacturing point to the customer. In online retailing, the supply chain usually represents the distributor and manufacturer of a product.

**Tracking Number:** An alphanumeric identification that shipping services like FedEx or the United States Postal Service assign to a specific package to facilitate monitoring and delivery confirmation.

**Trademark:** Government protection for words, symbols, or designs meant to represent a product or brand.

**Trade Show:** An exhibition created so that manufacturers and distributors may show or demonstrate new products or services.

**Traffic:** In Internet marketing, traffic represents the number of visitors a particular page or site receives.

**Usability:** The relative ease of navigating, reading, or otherwise interacting with a website or web application.

**Value Added Tax (VAT):** A tax added at each stage of a production process. Effectively, the tax applies each time "value" is added to the product.

**Vertical:** An industry segment made up of similar business and customers.

**VoIP:** Voice over Internet Protocol (VoIP) describes a set of technologies capable of enabling voice communications over an Internet connection rather than traditional telephone lines.

**Wholesale Price:** The price manufacturers, distributors, or other wholesalers charge retailers for products.

**Wholesaler:** A manufacturer, distributor, or similar that sells to retailers.

**XML:** The Extensible Markup Language or XML is a World Wide Web Consortium standard used to encode and annotate text documents. XML is frequently used in product feeds.

Made in United States
North Haven, CT
21 August 2022

22982307R00082